OSMOSIS
& Glassfibre
Yacht
Construction

OSMOSIS & Glassfibre Yacht Construction

SECOND EDITION

Tony Staton-Bevan

SHERIDAN HOUSE

Second edition
Published 1995 by
Sheridan House Inc.
145 Palisade Street
Dobbs Ferry, NY 10522

First published as *The Care and Repair of Glassfibre Yachts*
by Adlard Coles 1986
Revised and expanded edition entitled *Osmosis and the Care
and Repair of Glassfibre Yachts*
published by Sheridan House 1989

Library of Congress Cataloging-in-Publication Data

Staton-Bevan, Tony.
    Osmosis & glassfibre yacht construction/Tony Staton-Bevan.
    2nd ed.
        p.   cm.
    Rev. ed. of: Osmosis and the care and repair of glassfibre yachts.
    1989.
    Includes index.
    ISBN 0-924486-83-X
    1. Fiberglass boats–Maintenance and repair–Amateurs' manuals.
    I. Staton-Bevan, Tony. Osmosis and the care and repair of
    glassfibre yachts. II. Title
    VM321.S79 1995
    623.8'458–dc20   95–22044
                                                               CIP

Printed in Great Britain
ISBN 0-924486-83-X

Contents

Acknowledgements   vi
Preface   vii
Introduction to Second Edition   ix

1 Glass reinforced plastic construction   1
2 Gel coat blistering and osmosis   15
3 Hulls   47
4 Deck and coachroof   68
5 Fitting out   79
6 How to avoid osmosis and other types of blistering   106

Quick reference section – osmosis questions and answers   110
Glossary   115
Index   117

Acknowledgements

Photographs of mouldings etc., were kindly supplied by Halmatic Limited and Tyler Mouldings Limited.
Glassfibre materials were kindly supplied by Strand Glass Limited.

The author examining a blistered hull

Preface

The introduction of glass reinforced plastic (GRP) construction made it possible to build boats on a production line at far less cost than a one-off craft. This resulted in the start of the boating boom, by bringing the cost of boat ownership within the reach of millions of ordinary people, whereas 'Yachting' had previously been a rich man's sport.

Originally it was hailed as a wonder material which would be maintenance-free. It was even claimed that the bottom would be so smooth, no marine growth could attach itself and anti-fouling paint would not be required. That maintenance-free myth was soon dispelled, but even with all its faults, GRP requires less maintenance and can withstand more neglect and abuse than timber, steel or aluminium, which all deteriorate at a far greater rate. It has been said that this is the very problem with GRP craft, that they will not rot or corrode and that in the future there will be a glut of old and tatty GRP boats. To my mind this must be a good thing, for it will introduce even more people to boat ownership, due to the supply of older and therefore cheaper boats, on which DIY repairs can be carried out inexpensively. At present an old and cheap timber or steel vessel is likely to be suffering from rot and corrosion, which can be far more expensive to repair.

In this book I have described the most common forms of GRP construction and not only how to repair them but how to avoid unnecessary damage in the first place. It applies equally to a dinghy as to an off-shore cruiser, and to both power and sail.

Not only should it be of interest to the owner of a GRP craft, but the information will be invaluable to those thinking of buying one, since it may help to distinguish the good from the bad and also to the DIY builder who can avoid many of the common shortcomings.

While it is not intended to be a complete maintenance manual, I have covered the important areas peculiar to this form of construction and particularly those items which regularly appear on the defect list as I go about my day-to-day job as a yacht surveyor. However, it would be impossible to put into words everything I have learnt in 30 years of building and surveying and no matter how many books you might read, you cannot replace practical experience. For this reason I would strongly recommend that a qualified yacht surveyor is consulted before undertaking any major alterations or repair work. An hour of his time could save many of yours, not to mention the money you may be wasting by devaluing your boat.

This book will certainly help you to decide which surveyor is qualified to comment on GRP construction because, believe me, there are horses for courses and the man who is well versed on steel or timber is not always as good on GRP.

Introduction to the Second Edition

This completely revised second edition of the book covers the changes in building and repairing techniques over the last five years. One of the major advances has been the effect of better resins used in hull construction, which has reduced the ingress of moisture and resulted in a reduction in the development of blisters below the waterline.

Even more photographs have been added to this edition, detailing common failings found on glassfibre craft. I could just as easily have filled the pages with pictures of gleaming yachts and pointed out all the advantages of GRP construction – which, by the way, far outweigh any disadvantages. However, I hope that by describing the material, warts and all, it will provide a better understanding of glassfibre construction and how potential problems can be avoided or overcome.

The onset of gel coat blistering (osmosis) has caused many buyers to consider a timber instead of glassfibre vessel. The fact is that far worse defects are common in most wooden craft ten or more years old. After all, rectifying rot or corroded fastenings in a timber vessel can cost much more than treating osmosis which is also far less rapid in its advancement.

I can never understand why owners will happily strip and repaint the topsides on a wooden boat, but are scared to paint a glassfibre hull. I suppose they feel they have an affinity with timber, whereas glassfibre is something alien. This is great for boatyard business, but do bear in mind that it is much easier to paint onto gel coat because of its smooth, stable surface.

Perhaps it would help if one added up the maintenance costs on a wooden vessel over, say, ten years and compared them with those of a glassfibre vessel. One would find the former far in excess of the latter, even if blisters had to be repaired. 'But, ' I hear you say, 'I would carry out all the work on wood myself, not incurring large yard bills'. And this is my point: most work on GRP is relatively straightforward and easily within the capabilities of the average DIY owner.

Tony Staton-Bevan
1995

Chapter One

Glass reinforced plastic construction

During an external hull survey of a 40 foot GRP yacht, I spotted a small area of hairline cracks on the bottom, covering no more than a few square inches. At this point the boatyard foreman was passing so I asked him to look at the crazing before the boat was relaunched, as no doubt the owner would ask him to carry out a repair. He took a knife from his pocket, poked the cracks and decided that a simple repair to the gel coat was needed to prevent further ingress of water. I suggested that at the very least some reinforcement on the inside would be advisable. I received that all-too-familiar look, which often accompanies the statement about surveyors making mountains out of molehills, to justify their fees.

Although my original brief had been to examine just the outside of the hull for get coat blisters, in view of the cracks I thought it prudent to inspect the internal structure as well. I found the inside of the hull at this point was not readily accessible, but after removing access panels discovered that the small hairline cracks extended right through the $1/2$ inch (13 mm) thick hull and that slight leakage had occurred. Further examination revealed the glassfibre bonding on every bulkhead to be loose or cracked throughout the port side of the hull. Most of the longitudinal and transverse stiffeners were also cracked and movement of the port engine bearer meant that the propeller shaft was out of alignment.

The subsequent repair costs were considerable and yet the owner had been blissfully unaware of the problem and about to embark on an Atlantic crossing. He later admitted to an encounter with a submerged rock, but had been assured by a knowledgeable friend – who was navigating at the time – that the gentle bump had not caused any damage. But after all, even the boatyard foreman had recommended just a gel coat repair.

Thankfully, in this case the insurance company agreed to pay for the repairs, but it does demonstrate that a little knowledge of the construction and the likely effect of impact can be very useful, particularly to boat owners.

Glass reinforced plastic is the correct term used to describe this type of construction. The plastic is normally a liquid polyester resin, which is mixed with a catalyst (in this case a hardener) and used to saturate layers of cloth made from strands of glass fibres. When this has cured it forms a very strong laminate of resin and glass. It could be compared to concrete which is reinforced with steel rods. This form of construction is often known as glassfibre or fibreglass, although the latter is the trade-mark of a company producing glass fibre materials. In this book the laminated material will always be referred to as either GRP or glassfibre.

Without becoming too technical, in this chapter I will explain the most common methods of constructing GRP mouldings. By so doing I hope it will be easier to understand how and why defects occur and also how to repair them.

A length of glass fibre chopped strand mat is pulled from the roll and cut to size, ready for the laminator to lay up on the mould

Surface tissue – like a fine chopped strand mat

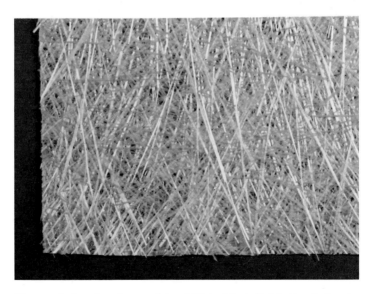

Chopped strand mat – consists of 1½ to 2 inch (3.8 to 5 cm) strands of glass fibre held in a random mat form by a PVA or polyester powder binder

Materials

All glass fibre mats, rovings and cloths come in rolls, just like other fabrics. In the same way that a dressmaker cuts out fabric from a pattern, a GRP laminator pre-cuts the lengths of glass fibre material to fit the shape of the hull – for instance, from the gunwale down to the keel.

A strand of glass fibre chopped strand mat (CSM) consists of a bundle of glass fibre filaments, each being thinner than a human hair. The chopped strands look a little like grass cuttings, except that they are white and held together by a binder which dissolves when resin is applied, making the CSM pliable and more easily rolled out into the complex curves and shapes.

Instead of cutting chopped strand mat from a roll, placing it in the mould and wetting out with resin, it is possible to carry out the same procedure from a special spray gun. It is fed with resin and a continuous length of glass roving, which resembles a ball of string. This is chopped into short lengths at the gun and sprayed into the mould with the resin, giving a chopped strand mat appearance. One drawback is the difficulty in maintaining a uniform thickness, but the speed at which a moulding can be laid up is an obvious attraction to many builders. It also permits a precise glass to resin ratio to be maintained.

Woven rovings consist of loosely woven, thicker continuous strands of glass fibre, a bit like twine. These provide greater strength and stiffness than the CSM and although not as strong as glass fibre cloth, the loose weave accommodates the complex shapes and it wets out fairly

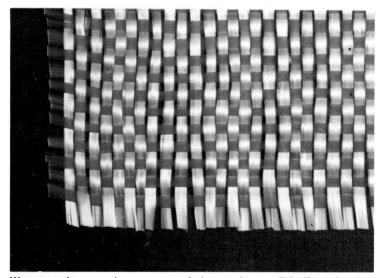

Woven rovings – a loose weave of glass rovings, a little like twine, but untwisted

Uni-directional rovings – again a loose weave but with a greater number running one way – to give greater strength in that direction. It is also available with all the fibres running in one direction, having loose stitching or tape to hold the rovings together

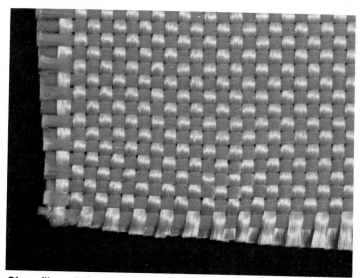

Glass fibre cloth – a tight weave of glass fibre which provides extra strength

well. Uni-directional rovings have a greater number of strands running in one direction and are used where greater strength is required in one direction. Both types should always be sandwiched between layers of CSM, otherwise there is a greater chance of air bubbles remaining in the thick weave. The tighter woven glass fibre cloth is sometimes used in areas of greater stress, such as above a keel, where extra strength is required.

In addition to glass fibre, hybrid materials can be used, although they are more common on racing yachts and power boats, where a high strength to low weight ratio is required. These include aramid (Kevlar) and carbon fibres. Ideally, on one-off boats, these materials are used in conjunction with an epoxy or vinylester laminating resin which is not only stronger, weight for weight, than polyester, but also have a better glue characteristic and adhere well to hybrid cloths as well as core materials such as foam or balsa, since sandwich construction is used extensively.

Almost all GRP production boats are constructed using polyester resin and predominantly glass fibre reinforcement, although Kevlar is sometimes used in highly stressed areas. To avoid any confusion, this book will be confined to dealing with the most common form of construction.

Hull moulding

To build a production boat, a mould is needed in which to construct – or lay up – the GRP moulding. To make a mould, a plug is needed. A plug, in the case of a hull, can simply be an existing hull from which a mould is taken. With a new production boat a prototype wooden hull might be built, but usually a plug is constructed as cheaply and simply as possible to achieve the desired hull shape.

This normally takes the form of frames set up on a level surface or strongback, over which battens are fastened to provide a fair surface. A thin wooden skin is applied over the battens, which is then filled, faired and painted. The amount of time and care taken at this stage is crucial, because any bumps, hollows or other imperfections will be transferred as a mirror image onto the mould and then onto every hull which is produced in it.

The mould is like a GRP hull laid up inside out, on top of the plug. It is a much heavier moulding than a normal hull, as it has to retain its shape for several years during which time many hulls will be laminated inside it. Before separating it from the plug a timber or steel framework is attached to the outside to form a supporting cradle.

After separation, the mould is polished to remove any minor imperfections and provide a perfectly smooth finish – or at least it should be!

Now it is ready for the first hull to be laid up. To prevent it from sticking to the mould, a release agent is applied over the whole of the inside

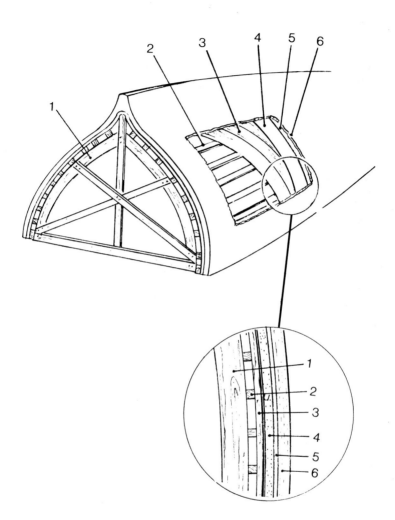

Plug and mould. The frames (1) are set up on a level surface, over which timber battens (2) are applied. Thin planks (3) are then attached diagonally to form the hull shape. The surface is filled (4) faired and painted to provide a perfectly smooth finish. The mould is then constructed over the top by applying gel coat (5) and sufficient layers of glassfibre and resin to provide a robust laminate (6)

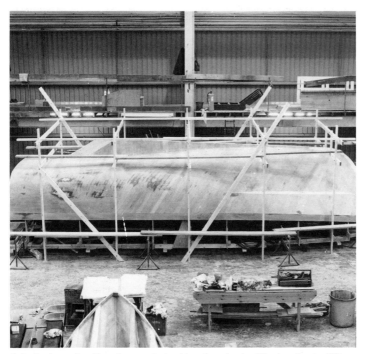

A hull plug after the diagonal planking has been fitted, prior to filling and painting

surface. Next the gel coat resin is brushed, or sprayed on. This is the pigmented polyester resin that provides a coloured and durable surface on the outside of the hull. Below the waterline an unpigmented (clear) gel coat resin is often used because pigments, particularly dark ones, make the gel coat more porous and therefore less waterproof. A clear coating also enables the underwater area to be checked visually for large voids or other defects, after it is moulded.

On top of the gel coat, it is important to apply a layer of powder-bound surface tissue, a very fine glassfibre mat, which is carefully laid onto a fresh coat of polyester resin, with further resin applied on top. This provides a resin rich back-up layer to the gel coat, which reduces the chances of voids, which would encourage water penetration and gel coat blistering. The gel coat should be an isophthalic or, isophthalic-NPG type and the first two layers of glassfibre reinforcement should be laminated using an isophthalic resin. (See page 25).

The rest of the hull is built up with successive layers of glassfibre chopped strand mat, often with alternate layers of woven rovings or glassfibre cloth, to provide additional rigidity and strength. A layer of Kevlar™ cloth may be used in areas of high stress. Each is laid in place over a fresh coat of resin, thoroughly wetted out with further resin and

A one-piece hull mould fitted with steel gimbals allowing it to be rolled from one side to the other to make access into the mould easier for the laminator. In the foreground two deck mouldings are being laid up, upside down

then consolidated with a roller. This encapsulates the glass fibres within the resin and thus produces a laminate of glass reinforced plastic.

Before removing the finished hull from the mould, any longitudinal stringers, transverse stiffeners, engine beds etc., are best fitted while the hull is evenly supported and in a 'green' semi-cured state.

As you can see, unlike timber, steel or alloy construction where the hull material is of a known quality, GRP is manufactured separately for each moulding and quality control is extremely important. If the resin and catalyst are not correctly proportioned and mixed, the resin will not attain its full strength. If the temperature is too low or humidity too high, again there will be a loss of strength. If too little resin is applied the moulding will be weak and prone to delamination. If any of the specified number of glassfibre laminations are omitted, the moulding will again be weak. So a good GRP laminator must be highly skilled. This was illustrated where I was asked to examine a six-month-old boat with blistered gel coat. I found that the port side was covered in one inch blisters below the waterline. The starboard side was in perfect condition. On visiting the builder's moulding shop I discovered that the hull was laid up in two halves, port and starboard, separately and then joined together, and furthermore, each half was being laid up by

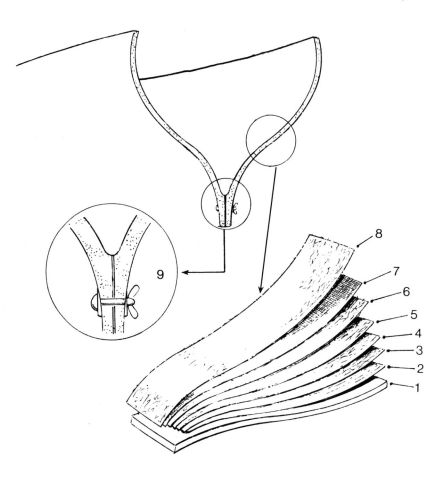

Hull laminate. The lay-up on a typical hull laminate will consist of gel coat resin applied to the mould (1), followed by surface tissue (2), layers of chopped strand mat (3)–(6), the number being dependent on the size of the hull and the strength required. At least one layer of woven rovings and/or glassfibre or Kevlar cloth (7) is normally included, followed by a final layer of CSM (8). Some hulls are laid up in a split mould (9) where inward slope such as tumblehome would not permit a moulding to be lifted from a one-piece mould. It is sometimes also done just to make the laminator's job easier

With all the glass fibre material cut to length the laminator places them in the correct position and applies polyester resin with a brush until completely saturated. He then uses a metal roller to consolidate the glass fibre and tease out any visible air bubbles

a different laminator. I do not know if the manager had records to show who laminated the port side of the defective hull, but it does demonstrate how the same materials used under the same conditions rely on the skill of the laminator.

Deck moulding

The construction of a plug for the deck mould is similar to that of the hull but much more complex, since it normally incorporates not only the decks, but the coachroof and cockpit as well. The positioning of hatch openings, raised pads for deck fittings and often a non-slip deck surface, all have to be accommodated.

Once a mould has been made from the plug, a deck moulding can be laid up. This is similar to laying up a hull except that on most boats the relatively flat horizontal surfaces are stiffened by a sandwich construction. The sandwich consists of two skins of GRP laminate with rigid expanded foam or end grain balsa between them. (See page 76). This is a very efficient way of providing the rigidity required to take the crew's weight without laying up a thicker and therefore heavy moulding, or fitting beams on the underside, which are not as effective.

While the hull is still supported in the mould a section of ballast is low-ered into the keel section. Also note the longitudinal stringers being fit-ted

After the release agent, gel coat and a few layers of chopped strand mat and resin, the sheets of foam or balsa, normally about $1/2$ inch (13 mm) thick, are cut to size and bonded down on resin. It is important at this stage to determine where fittings will be through-bolted, and in these areas hardwood or plywood pads are substituted, since the soft core would be crushed when the bolts are tightened. Further layers of CSM, woven rovings and resin are then laid up on top of the core to com-plete the deck moulding.

The hull and deck construction described here are the most common types. Sandwich construction, similar to that on the deck moulding, is sometimes used for the hull and can provide a very strong and light structure. Its drawbacks include the possibility of delamination and minor damage leading to ingress of water into the core. One-off, as opposed to production boats, are usually built over a plug in a similar way to a mould, except that the outer surface of the moulding is filled and faired to a smooth finish and then painted.

Gel coat being brushed and rolled onto the inverted deck mould

Interior mouldings

In addition to the hull and deck there are often a number of other mould-ings which fit inside the boat.

The most common one incorporates the cabin sole, bunks, lockers and sometimes the galley, washbasins, engine bearers, etc. From the builder's point of view this can save weeks of fitting out work where the same areas have to be constructed in timber for each boat. Although these interior mouldings were common in the 1970s, there has been a move away from the cold impersonal look of gel coat surfaces. Some builders have returned to timber joinery, often built on a jig elsewhere and simply lowered into the hull before the deck is attached. Others still incorporate a GRP moulding but attach timber panels and fabrics to improve the appearance. On most boats it is an important part of the structure and together with the bulkheads, is used to stiffen and sup-port the hull. A few manufacturers inject the foam between the interior moulding and the hull to provide buoyancy and additional stiffness.

A well designed interior moulding is an ingenious piece of engineer-ing, incorporating everything from the engine bearers and keel stiffen-ing to the toilet-roll holder. Where it incorporates the use of timber and fabric linings it can be both practical and attractive.

A headlining moulding was also common and usually fitted up under the deck moulding to provide a smooth finish and reduce condensation. Here again, many manufacturers have changed to less austere fabric linings. Where fitted, a glassfibre headlining is rarely designed to provide any support but is merely a thin cosmetic moulding.

A layer of CSM and woven rovings being laid up in the mould. Note how the white glassfibres in the CSM on the right become translucent when wetted out with resin on the left. The laminator is using a metal roller to consolidate the glassfibre/resin laminate, having applied the resin from the bucket with a roller and brush.
Note: Resin must be applied first with the glassfibre reinforcement laid over the wet resin, so that it soaks through from behind. This reduces the likelihood of air being trapped in the laminate, creating a potential for osmotic blistering

Chapter Two

Gel coat blistering and osmosis

Although it was first widely acknowledged 20 years ago, this is still the subject most talked about by owners of glassfibre yachts, and with good reason, for there are few other repairs that can cost a large percentage of the boat's value without being covered by an insurance policy. In the USA, gel coat blistering is often known as 'box pox', while in Europe it is called 'osmosis'. Both tend to be used as all-embracing terms to describe anything from a minute pimple to a swelling several inches across. In reality, blisters have different causes which can normally be identified by their shape.

Osmotic blister

The true osmotic blister is caused by a natural process known as osmosis. This is where a fluid of a lower density is drawn through a porous membrane to a fluid of a higher density, in an attempt to equalise the density of the two fluids. Trees transmit water from their roots to the leaves in this way. In the case of a glassfibre hull the fluid of a lower density is the water in which it floats, the porous membrane is the gel coat and a void within the hull contains the fluid of a higher density.

Unfortunately, all gel coats are porous to a greater or lesser extent, but why voids filled with a dense fluid? The voids are air bubbles trapped during the moulding process, as it is almost impossible to eliminate all air from the moulding no matter how carefully it is laminated. Often trapped within these air bubbles are substances such as unreacted resin curing agents and the binding material used to hold the glass fibres together in a mat formation. Water molecules pass through the gel coat and form droplets within the voids. Here they dissolve out the soluble substances, to create a dense liquid. At this point osmosis takes over and draws the water molecules through the gel coat at a much faster rate. When a void has been filled, the process continues, pressure builds up and a blister is formed. Eventually the pressure may

A typical case of osmosis where blisters up to ½ inch (13 mm) in diameter are visible on the surface of the gel coat after removal of several square feet of anti-fouling paint

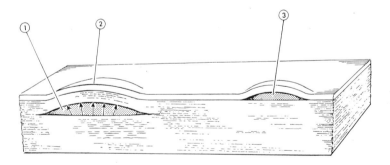

Osmosis. Where moisture permeates through to a void (1) deep in the hull, the subsequent osmotic pressure can cause delamination and will show up as a large blister or swelling on the surface (2). This is unusual and the most common type of osmotic blister forms between the gel coat and first layer of glassfibre reinforcement (3)

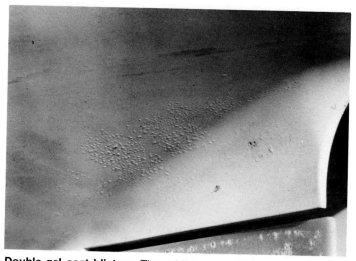

Double gel coat blisters. These blisters are fairly distinctive, being found in closely spaced rashes, with many following almost straight lines

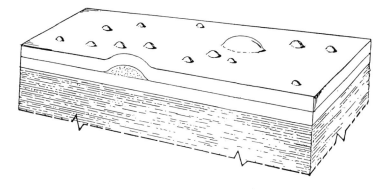

Double gel coat. With the acceptance of gel coat blistering in the 1970s, some manufacturers produced hulls (and some do so now) with a double gel coat to provide a thicker, more water resistant coating. However, it is common to find blisters forming at the interface between the two layers

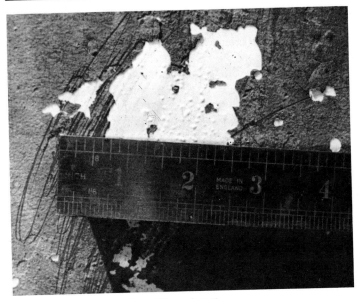

Blisters caused by aeration of the gel coat

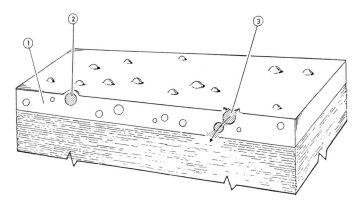

Aeration of the gel coat. When mixing the gel coat resin with the catalyst or apply-ing it to the mould, it is possible for air bubbles to be incorporated if either function is carried out too vigorously. When it has cured this results in the gel coat having an appearance similar to Gruyère cheese (1). Moisture quickly permeates into those bubbles near the surface (2) and osmotic pressure can cause a blister to form. Due to the greater porosity caused by the aeration, moisture can also per-meate through to the laminate (3) with greater ease. This condition is also common where get coat is sprayed into the mould, resulting in millions of minute air bubbles which often appear on the surface of deck mouldings as craters or pin-holes, which are highlighted when dirt collects in them

crack the gel coat allowing the liquid to escape, or the density of the water within the blister will be equalised with that outside and this plus a slight weakening of the gel coat will often allow the fluid to permeate back out through the gel coat when the vessel is ashore.

Osmotic blisters are normally (2 mm to 100 mm) circular in shape and can be anything from $^1/16$ inch up to several inches in diameter. When pierced, the pungent smelling, normally acidic liquid is unmistakable. However, as I have already described, it is possible to have just a damp or dry blister when the process has run its course. Dry blisters can also be caused by gases produced as a result of a chemical reaction within the laminate. The most common type of blister is normally formed just below the gel coat, where air has been trapped beneath or within the first layer of glassfibre reinforcement. These blisters are usually between $^1/16$ inch and $^1/2$ inch (2 mm and 13 mm) in diameter. They rarely cause a serious structural defect although further ingress of water through the blister cavity should be prevented, because the acidic liquid created can slowly degrade, and therefore weaken, the laminate.

Less common are larger osmotic blisters, several inches in diameter, which form deep in the laminate and in this case can cause large areas of delamination and build up pressures as high as 60 psi. I can vouch for this, having had to avoid being sprayed with liquid on many occasions when piercing this form of blister.

Another common type of blister is that found within or between the layers or gel coat. Such blisters are normally between $^1/16$ inch and $^1/4$ inch (2 mm and 6 mm) in diameter and are found in closely-spaced rashes, which can eventually cover the whole of the underwater area. These occur due to a similar osmotic process when air bubbles are trapped in the gel coat during its application to the mould. They have little or no effect on the structure but a protective coating must be applied to replace the damaged gel coat, which would otherwise permit ingress of water at a faster rate.

Dry voids

Blisters should not be confused with an ordinary dry void in the moulding where no blister has formed. These are quite common and owners of glassfibre craft will probably have found them on the deck moulding, particularly on sharp corners. These occur where large pockets of air are trapped, due to insufficient consolidation of the glass fibre reinforcement when the hull is being moulded and do not necessarily weaken the moulding. If they contain no moisture and the glassfibre does not have a dry, resin-starved appearance, they can be filled with gel coat resin, or if more than $^1/16$ inch (2 mm) deep, an epoxy filler, followed by gel coat resin. If, however, there is an area of dry glass, this will have to be cut out and relaminated.

Clearly visible here are the distinctive pear-shaped blisters and ridges formed on the surface of the white gel coat, by wicking. They are sometimes referred to as fibre aligned blisters, since they follow the random pattern of the chopped strand mat. Opening sample blisters reveals the swollen fibres underneath

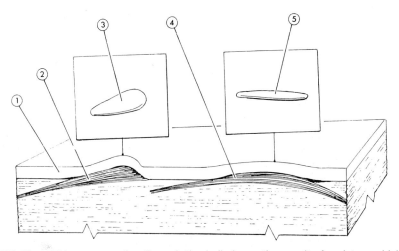

Wicking. This cross-section through the hull shows the result of moisture which has permeated through the gel coat (1) and penetrated individual strands of glass fibre. This causes them to swell up and distort the surface of the gel coat. A strand (2) with its end close to, or often embedded in the gel coat, forms a pear-shaped blister on the surface (3). Where the centre of a strand (4) is closer to the surface, a long ridge is formed (5)

Wicking

The other common type of blistering, often wrongly called osmosis, is that caused by wicking. This occurs when moisture permeates through the gel coat and is then drawn down the glass fibres by capillary attraction. Each strand is made up from dozens of smaller glass fibres, and these are not always completely wetted out by the relatively viscous resin and thus form ideal capillary tubes. The moisture within these strands causes them to swell up and break away from the surrounding resin. On the surface of the gel coat they appear as elongated blisters or ridges which follow the random pattern of the glass fibre chopped strand mat. If left over a period of years, this ingress of moisture can progress deeper into the moulding causing serious delamination, which weakens the hull considerably – I have seen more than $1/4$ inch (7 mm) of a hull delaminated where the total thickness was less than $1/2$ inch (13 cm) If a hull in this condition suffers even relatively minor impact, it is much more likely to fracture. Wicking is graphically illustrated when the hull is moulded below the waterline with clear gel coat. Instead of

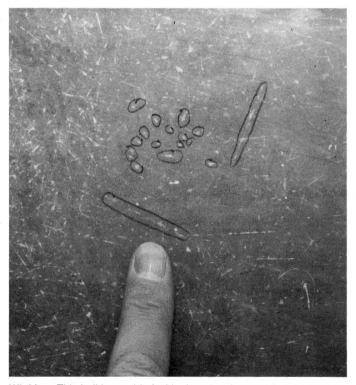

Wicking. This hull is moulded with clear (unpigmented) gel coat resin below the waterline. The swollen strands show up clearly as white lines; a few have been circled above my finger

being translucent, the individual strands are visible as white lines, where their bond with the resin has been broken.

Which hulls suffer from blistering? The answer is that at present no gel coat is totally waterproof and therefore all GRP hulls can soak up water. All you then need are glass fibres which are not completely wetted out with resin, or have cavities with soluble substances present, and you have the potential for wicking or osmosis, or both! This description probably applies to 98% of all glassfibre craft. Regrettably, the only sure way to determine whether any one boat has the potential would be to take core samples from several areas of the hull and have them analysed. But even then, the chemists do not seem to have all the answers.

My own figures show that of all the GRP craft I survey, currently around 250 a year, 30–35% suffer from blistering of some kind. On craft 10 to 12 years old, the figure jumps to around 60%. One positive factor, is that on vessels moulded over the last seven years, where better quality resins, such as isophthalic, have been incorporated into the two outer laminates, these have shown greatly reduced blistering and ingress of moisture into the laminate. (See page 25)

Boats kept in fresh water or warm water are likely to blister much sooner and it is not unusual to find blistering after 12 months afloat under either of these conditions, where the less waterproof orthophthalic resins are used. The reason is that fresh water has a lower density than salt water, which increases the osmotic pressure, causing water molecules to permeate through the gel coat more quickly. Tests have shown that the rate of water penetration through gel coat *doubles* for every 18°F (8°C) increase in water temperature. The warmer water not only softens the gel coat, making it more permeable, but also accelerates any chemical reaction. This is why blistering is so common in the warmer water of the Mediterranean, Caribbean and more southerly parts of the USA, where the climatic conditions are ideal for boating but disastrous for a glassfibre hull. In the summer, the northern European waters rarely reach more than 55°F–60°F (13°C–16°C) whereas the Mediterranean is around 78°F (25°C) and the Caribbean and Florida are around 85°F–90°F (29°C–32°C). As you can see, when compared with northern European waters, the same boat kept in the Mediterranean will suffer water penetration at twice the rate and if taken across the Atlantic to, say, Miami, the rate is almost quadrupled.

It is on those craft which have been kept in warmer waters that I most commonly find large blisters deep in the laminate which, when pierced, emit a quantity of dark, vile-smelling liquid. With one such boat, I placed my Barcol impressor on the hull to measure the hardness of the gel coat and it would not register. After cursing the airline with whom I had travelled the previous day, who must surely have dropped my case containing the instrument, I tested in on the boat alongside. It immediately registered 41, which is the average reading for a gel coat in good condition. I then took readings in several areas on the boat being surveyed and the highest was 10, which was obtained on the topsides, suggesting that there was an inherent defect. There was very little doubt that a gel coat this soft would be very porous and would have blistered even in a cooler climate.

Less common blistering

Most cases of blistering occur below and up to a few inches above the waterline. However, the first cases of osmotic blistering that I saw were in the 1960s, in glassfibre water tanks which were often built into the keel section of a yacht. The inside of the keel moulding was painted with gel coat to form the bottom and sides, and a glassfibre lid formed the top. From my own statistics I now of course know that fresh water is more likely to cause blistering. Even today I still come across cases of blistering in water tanks, but thankfully less tanks are currently made of glassfibre.

When I was asked to examine a GRP hydrotherapy pool at a large hospital, I was not surprised to find that it was suffering from severe osmotic blistering, 12 months after installation – not, that is, when I discovered that the fresh water was maintained at a temperature of 95°F (35°C). What is surprising is that the hospital administrators with all their learned advisors did not anticipate the problem which had been well known to swimming pool manufacturers for at least 15 years and hence the reason that they no longer use glass/polyester laminates in their construction.

Gel coat blistering more than a few inches above the waterline is fairly rare. However, there are exceptions. I know of one sailing yacht used for extended cruising which would often spend days or sometimes weeks on one tack with a large area of the lee topsides underwater for long periods, in warmer waters. She eventually developed small osmotic blisters well above the waterline in these immersed areas.

Air bubbles within the gel coat – which are more commonly found in darker shades, due to the higher viscosity caused by the pigments – can appear as blisters when the topsides are exposed to hot sun. This is due to the heat expanding the air inside them, and they normally contract and disappear when in the shade.

In a few isolated cases, often where a vessel is in very damp conditions with fresh water constantly running down the topsides, I have seen extensive osmotic blistering extending from the waterline to the gunwale. Once again this is normally due to aeration in the gel coat. There have also been cases of deeper osmosis and of wicking on the topsides, but this has been because of a major fault in the moulding process.

It is important to make sure that water does not lie on the decks when a vessel is laid up ashore, as blistering is possible if the water remains there for long periods of time. I have also seen blistering in the gel coat of a berth moulding where water from a deck leak remains unnoticed under a berth cushion. Another common area for blistering inside a boat is under a flexible water tank, which can be due to a leak in the tank or just condensation which often occurs there.

There is one final danger to avoid, particular;y when a GRP craft is stored ashore for long periods. If the keel or keels are glassfibre with internal ballast, make sure that they are not standing in a pool of fresh water – a puddle of water in the sun becomes very warm. If the hull is supported by a cradle or shores, a timber wedge or chock, especially if padded with carpet or foam, will retain moisture and I have seen quite serious blistering occur around supports, particularly on new hulls which have been ashore for several years whilst the owners fit them out.

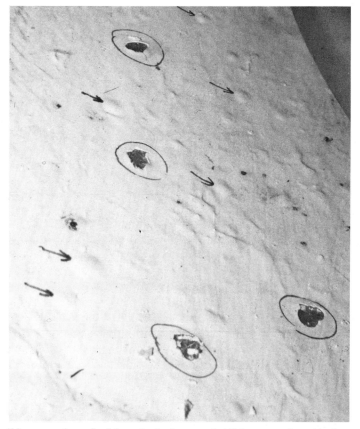

After removing a flexible water tank, osmotic blisters were found in the layer of gel coat painted over the inside of the hull. Some are indicated by the arrows, the ones circled were opened and found to contain liquid. These were caused just by the condensation that formed between the water tank and the hull. A piece of plywood or some other form of insulation should have been used

Conclusions

Since it is possible to become paranoid about the 'disease' it is important to keep it in perspective. If the early stages of blistering are found,
it is obviously prudent to carry out some form of remedial treatment
before the condition worsens or causes serious structural damage.
However, the passage of water into the hull moulding is normally a very
slow process and it takes many years of water absorption before any significant weakness occurs in the structure. The exception is where extensive blistering occurs during the first two or three years of a boat's life.
Research has shown that in some cases this is an indication of an inherent moulding defect, such as substandard resin or incomplete curing. It
also follows that if blisters appear in the early life of a hull, the condition
is likely to progress at a much faster rate than one which has taken 10
years to exhibit the problem.

The actual process of osmosis and wicking has been simplified here,
because it is a subject which alone could easily fill a book. The chemical reactions and hydrolysis which can occur within a GRP hull are very
complex, but for the average boat owner, they are purely academic.
What is of real interest is how it can be avoided or if it has occurred,
how can it be treated.

Prevention and treatment of blistering

Prevention

If we accept that many glassfibre craft will suffer at some time, then say-
ing 'prevention is better than cure' has never been more true. It is also
far cheaper than waiting for blistering to occur. Of course, the first line
of defence lies with the moulder. Available to him are a wide range of
resins and reinforcing materials. Research carried out on both sides of
the Atlantic has shown that Isophthalic (Iso) acid-based polyester
resins are less likely to blister than the more commonly used
Orthophthalic (Ortho) acid-based polyester resins. For even better
resistance an Isophthalic-Neopentyl Glycol (Iso-NPG) resin is available.
With the glassfibre chopped strand mat (CSM) it has long been known
that in the commonly used mat, where the strands are held in a mat
form by a polyvinyl acetate (PVA) emulsion binder, these mats are more
likely to cause blistering than those employing a polyester powder
binder.

Although the majority of moulders now use an iso gel coat, many
have been very reluctant to change over to an Iso-resin and the use of
Iso-NPG gel coat or laminating resin is very rare.

However, a number of factors have changed the situation in Europe.
Hundreds of Beneteau yachts built in the early 1980s developed blisters
due to the supply of a faulty catalyst to this French mass production
builder. Around the same period, other builders were going through a
lean time and, amongst other things, found cheaper resin suppliers. It is

no coincidence that blisters started to appear on these hulls after as little as one-and-a-half to two years.

In order to regain the boating public's confidence extended warranties against osmosis, of up to ten years, became fairly common. It is no surprise that many of these have been made possible by the use of an Iso-gel coat, plus two layers of powder-bound CSM laid up using ISO or other high quality resins, such as Bisphenolic or Epacryn 'modified epoxy'.

My own experience with hulls which have been moulded with an Iso-gel coat and as little as one layer of CSM laid up with an Iso-resin is very encouraging. After seven years afloat ingress of moisture has been reduced by 70% and blistering is almost non-existent.

In the days of timber construction one had a choice of different types of wood and if an owner required the best he could specify teak planking instead of pine or mahogany. The different types of timber can be compared to the modern-day materials, such as Ortho, Iso and Iso-NPG, but the price differential is far less than those on the different types of timber.

As can be seen, when ordering a new boat it is well worth checking on the materials to be used. Failing this, a protective coating can be applied over the gel coat below the waterline, in order to minimise water penetration.

At present epoxy based paints seem to offer the best protection, due to their superior adhesive qualities and resistance to water penetration. Although in the past solvent-based epoxy paints have proved fairly reliable, to achieve an effective water barrier requires a build up of at least four coats of paint. In doing this it is possible for solvents to be trapped within the coating, or even in the hull itself, which can result in the epoxy remaining soft and being less waterproof. In my experience and that of the paint companies, the failure of many epoxy coatings could be attributed to solvent entrapment. In most cases this was due to maintaining insufficient temperatures or incorrect overcoating intervals, but the fact remains that solvents were the real cause. It is also a fact that solvents in other types of marine paints, even anti-fouling paint, can migrate into the hull, particularly where there is a substandard gel coat.

Further research and development by paint companies led to the production of solvent-free epoxy paints. These products have many advantages. They can be applied at up to $^8/_{1000}$ of an inch (200 microns) per coat and, since they contain no solvent, the wet and dry film thicknesses are virtually the same. Many solvent-based epoxy paints have a dry film thickness of less than half that when wet. In other words, for every litre pack you buy, more than half disappears into the atmosphere or, even worse, it may migrate into the hull, which you have dried out so carefully. With solvent-free epoxy, successive coats can be applied as soon as the preceding one is touch-dry, with no fear of impeding the curing process. The working environment is also more pleasant, without the strong smell of solvents, although good ventilation is still recommended.

To obtain an effective protective coating hulls must be clean and dry. With a new hull this is simple, as the only preparation required is to degrease and abrade the surface. However, it is important to ensure that the moulding has fully cured and this may take as long as two (or more) months, depending on the type of resins used and the temperature maintained during the curing period. An older boat will almost certainly have a layer of anti-fouling paint and has probably absorbed some moisture. As a matter of interest, a thick build up of anti-fouling paint will provide some protection against ingress of moisture, although it is not technically a waterproof coating. When anti-fouling paints containing TBT were banned in Europe it was found that some of the new anti-foulings were incompatible and many owners decided to remove all the coatings back to the gel coat, to overcome the incompatibility problem and also obtain a smoother finish on the hull. However, I have discovered numerous cases where this has been the direct cause of the development of gel coat blisters within as little as 12 months. The moral of this story is simple. Do not remove many years' build up of anti-fouling paint unless you intend to apply a protective epoxy coating.

Unless the anti-fouling paint has very poor adhesion, careful grit-blasting is the simplest way to remove it, as the use of paint remover tends to be a very long and messy job. Grit-blasting also abrades the surface, giving a good mechanical bond for the paint. After removing anti-fouling it is important to check that the hull is completely blister-free. Even if there are only a few blisters, these must be opened up. The

Careful grit-blasting carried out by a specialist will remove the layer of anti-fouling paint and leave the gel coat lightly abraded to provide a perfect key for a protective epoxy coating. Concentrating on one spot for a longer period will remove the gel coat if required

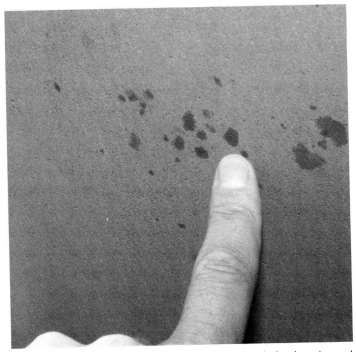

After sand-blasting this hull – note the lightly abraded gel coat – wet patches became visible on the surface the following day. These are caused by small voids full of water which could be latent osmotic cells. They must be opened up, washed out and dried out prior to painting

hull is then washed down thoroughly with fresh water to remove any impurities.

The next step is to dry out the hull. This can be a long process and, unless you are willing to be without the boat for at least a couple of months in the summer, it is best done over the winter. In either case, if the vessel is outside, the underwater area must be protected from rain. This can be achieved by covering the whole boat or just taping a polythene skirt around the waterline to deflect rainwater. Remember also to fit short lengths of pipe in the cockpit or deck drain outlets so that the water runs clear of the hull.

When dry – a moisture meter will measure this – painting can start. The number of coats required will depend on the dry film thickness of each coat of paint. In my experience a total build-up of something like $^{16}/_{1000}$ inch (400 microns) is needed, and anything thinner than this is less likely to be successful. Also remember to take the coating at least three inches (75 mm) above the waterline, in case the boat is ever trimmed incorrectly. Coating must be carried out in fairly warm conditions and when the atmosphere is not too humid. Most epoxies stop curing at around 40°F (4°C) and if solvent-based products have not

Moisture meter on wicking. 1 Note the fairly high moisture reading registered when a simple electronic moisture meter is placed over an area of wicking visible through the clear gel coat. This must be opened up and dried out before painting commences

2 When the meter is moved across to the translucent and therefore sound area of the hull the reading is nil. Although this is visually obvious when a clear gel coat has been used, with a pigmented one the use of a moisture meter is imperative.
Note: a more sophisticated meter would probably detect a low level of moisture

sufficiently cured before applying subsequent coats, there will be solvent entrapment which can cause blistering and softness of the coating
at a later date. Solvent-free epoxy may be applied as soon as the preceding coat is touch-dry.

Both types of paint are normally overcoated with an anti-fouling
primer or the anti-fouling paint within a few hours of the last coat of
epoxy, to ensure a chemical bond. Timing is critical and the paint manufacturer's instructions should be followed carefully. In fact this applies
throughout the coating procedure, because unlike some other paints,
the mixing, application and temperature are important if the coating is
to attain its full strength and provide an effective water barrier. An
added complication is that each paint manufacturer has a different set
of instructions, each applicable to his particular formulation of resins
and catalyst; some permit launching within a few days, others require
up to two weeks, although all are dependent on temperature.

Laboratory tests

Over the last ten years, various tests have been carried out in labora-
tories to prove the effectiveness or otherwise of different types of
paint coatings, which can be applied to hulls as prevention against, or
treatment for, gel coat blistering. Over the last 18 years, I have been
closely involved with the application and subsequent success of
numerous different types of paint coating, the majority of which have
been epoxy (epoxide) based. In almost every case, the results of the
laboratory tests have been contrary to my own findings when the
coatings are applied to real boats under real environmental conditions. It would appear that there are two reasons for the variance
between the controlled tests and those under real conditions. Firstly,
many of the tests are carried out under what are termed 'accelerated
conditions'. This is where the water temperatures are increased to
speed up the likely breakdown of the coatings. However in my experience, the same coatings react in an entirely different way when
exposed to lower water temperatures over a number of years. In
almost all cases, they tend to be more reliable and longer lasting.
Secondly, the two component paints can be mixed with exactly the
right ratios and applied under ideal conditions in a laboratory. The
reverse is often the case when these are applied under boatyard conditions and those coatings which are more tolerant to less exacting
standards often perform better.

My experience and that of others, is that a solvent-free epoxy coating
of at least $^{16}/_{1000}$ inch (400 microns) is required for protection and at least
$^{24}/_{1000}$ inch (600 microns) for treatment, after the gel coat is removed, and
these are proving to be very effective. Where it has been correctly
applied, under the right conditions, I have experienced a 90% success
rate over a period of ten years. This is undoubtedly why many of the
paint manufacturers can now offer a five year insurance backed warranty on these coatings. Only time will tell how long the coatings will

Gel plane. One of the new generation of hand held electric gel coat planers. Vertical sections of gel coat, the width of the planer head, are removed without damaging the glass fibre laminate underneath

On this close up of another hand-held planer one of the cutters on the rotating head can be seen. It also shows the suction hose which removes most of the 'peeled' gel coat

ultimately last, but from my own findings to date, I would suggest that it may be 8 to 10 years, after which period they will probably need to be replaced. However wintering ashore will increase their life.

Treatment

Those owners who have an adequate thickness of epoxy paint applied properly to a dry hull can be fairly confident that blisters will not form for many years. But what about the boat with blisters? If there are only a few, small isolated areas – up to 10% of the underwater area – these can be opened up, washed out and treated as I have described, except that the blister craters are filled with epoxy filler. If more of the hull is affected, then total removal of the gel coat below the waterline is advisable. This is the only way to get to the root of the problem. If water molecules have penetrated the gel coat and dissolved out any soluble substances, there will be latent osmotic cells and these must be washed out and dried thoroughly, otherwise blisters will form in the epoxy coating – as you would expect if a damp piece of wood were painted, but in this case, further complicated by the substances present. If moisture remains, the other problem is that hydrolysis may occur within the laminate, which could result in a slow but gradual weakening of the moulding.

The first stage of the treatment is the removal of the gel coat from the underwater area and to a line three inches (75 mm) above the waterline, or higher than this if the blistering extends above it. This can be done by using a gel coat planer, by grit-blasting or by grinding.

At the time of writing, another method being developed in Sweden is the HYAB Osmosis Lance technique. HYAB is short for Hyper Absorption. This is where a propane heated lance is used together with a jet of cold air to heat the affected areas of the hull laminate and vaporise moisture and other contaminants within the laminate. The inventors of this method state that whilst this leaves a damaged laminate, it is subsequently reinforced again, by saturating it with a low viscosity resin. At the time of writing, this process has not been widely used. I still have to be convinced that it is both safe and effective, whilst other tried and tested methods are being used successfully.

By far the most popular current form of gel coat removal is to use a gel coat peeler or planer. The original peeler developed in Holland is a complex piece of equipment with a remotely operated robotic arm, as shown on the front cover of this book. This was found to be a very efficient way of removing the gel coat, as the cutter blades can be adjusted to a preset depth. In this way, it is possible to remove just the gel coat, without removing the hull laminate and thus reducing the strength of the hull. However it was soon found that this gel coat peeler, whilst an ingenious invention, was expensive to buy, and also cumbersome and restrictive, since it had to be set up on rails alongside the hull. It was not long before smaller hand-held machines were developed and these have been gradually refined over the last few years. Today, the most

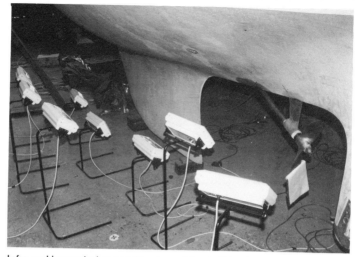

Infra-red lamps being used to dry out the hull laminate after removal of the gel coat. The hull temperature must be monitored to prevent over-heating. Self-adhesive thermometer strips can be used to maintain this below about 130°F (54°C)

Dehumidifier in use. The dehumidifier – in this case a small model – is encapsulated with polythene under the boat

popular are the hand-held electric planers which are small and versatile enough to remove the gel coat from irregular shaped sections of the hull.

Once a sample section of the gel coat has been removed, the cutter depth guide is set to the thickness of the gel coat, which is then removed in vertical strips about three inches (75 mm) wide. This is obviously a skilled job and requires a considerable amount of training and experience, as well as physical strength. It is also important that the blades are changed regularly, as they can leave an uneven or ragged surface when they become worn. However when carried out by an experienced operator, the gel coat will be removed cleanly, leaving a smooth fair surface. This is one of the main benefits when using a gel coat planer, in that it retains the original profile of the hull, which will not require any time-consuming, extensive filling and fairing afterwards. One potential drawback with this method is that it does not identify and search out any deeper seated blisters or pockets of moisture in the same way that grit-blasting will. However, to remove the hard outer shell of the gel coat, the grit-blasting contractor must use considerable pressure, but once the grit has broken through the gel coat, it will often cause unnecessary damage to the softer underlying glassfibre laminate. If the gel coat is first removed with a gel coat planing machine, the grit-blasting can then be carried out in a far more controlled manner, at a lower pressure, to open up moisture filled voids and deeper blisters, without causing unnecessary damage and destroying the overall profile of the vessel.

I have found that a few boatyards use a gel coat peeler or planing machine, but are reluctant to lightly grit-blast the surface afterwards. This has left moisture-filled voids – possible latent osmotic cells – unexposed below the surface. If these are not removed, there is a risk that they will cause the epoxy coating to fail at a later date. Unfortunately, it is not possible to distinguish between the thousands of harmless dry air bubbles and those which contain moisture, and the most effective way to open up all these voids is to lightly grit-blast the surface. Whilst this will partially destroy the relatively smooth surface left by the gel coat peeler, it does overcome another major problem, that of drying the hull. A smooth 'planed' surface will inhibit the drying process, whereas a pitted or cratered surface will aid the drying by presenting a much larger surface area and provide a superior mechanical key for the epoxy paint and filler.

On an older hull, where blistering has been left unchecked, it is not uncommon to find blisters as deep as $3/16$ inch (5 mm) below the surface. In this case, heavier grit-blasting will seek out the deeper seated blisters. In a really severe case, it is possible to get both blisters and delamination well below the surface. This will often occur along a line of woven rovings or cloth, where the interlaminar adhesion is not as good as between two layers of chopped strand mat. In such cases, it has been possible to progressively cut away the outer layers with the gel coat planer until sound laminate is reached. When doing this, it is very important to ensure that the weakened hull is adequately supported so that it does not sag or become distorted where the thickness is dramatically reduced. After removing the outer laminate of a hull, it is obviously necessary to replace the equivalent thickness with new laminate. I would normally recommend that this is carried out using glassfibre cloth and a vinylester or epoxy laminating resin, to provide the highest possible strength. When carrying out such a major repair, a skilled work force is required. Any joints between the old and new laminate should have a 12:1 taper. Of course, it will not always be found necessary to remove the outer laminate from the whole of the hull. If the interlaminar blisters are not widespread, it is quite possible to repair these individually after forming a shallow taper around the edge of each affected section. Before carrying out any of these repairs, it will be necessary to thoroughly wash and dry the hull as described later in this chapter.

When the resin has fully cured, it must be coarsely abraded and degreased to provide a good mechanical bond. It is then possible to proceed with the epoxy paint and filler as described later in this chapter.

When a gel coat planer is not available, grit-blasting may be used for removing blistered gel coat. An experienced operator will normally leave a relatively smooth surface. Beware of the inexperienced grit-blaster who may not remove sufficient gel coat or may, on the other hand leave the hull considerably weakened and looking like the surface of the moon! Indeed, I have seen many cases where a contractor used to working on steel, has blown holes right through the hull!

Another common method, is removal with a coarse grinding disc on an electric drill or an angle-grinder and, since no expensive equipment or sub-contractor is required, it is favoured by the do-it-yourself owner. The major drawback I have encountered with this method is that the grinding disc tends to heat up and seal the surface, although this can be overcome by reducing the speed to less than 1000 rpm. Also, as with the gel coat planer, it will not seek out deeper blisters. I would not normally recommend this form of gel coat removal except in cases of minor blistering where the laminate is relatively dry.

Assuming that the gel coat comes off easily and that the laminate underneath is sound, then ideally the hull should be hot pressure washed several times over seven days, to remove all acids and other contaminants. If a hot pressure wash is not available, a suitable unit or steam cleaning equipment should be hired. The next stage is to dry out the hull. One method is to use infra-red lamps. Those which have proved effective in drying out the glassfibre laminate incorporate a 1500 watt quartz short wave infra-red tube. One with a multi-facet reflector will be more effective than a conventional semi-circular reflector, as the latter tends to produce hot and cold spots rather than an even heat pattern. Great care must be exercised when using these lamps as most common resins will begin to degrade at around 131°F (55°C). Roughly speaking, this means that if the hull is too hot to keep the palm of your hand on it, it is too hot! If in doubt, a surface temperature measuring thermometer should be used.

If a safe temperature is maintained there should not be any problems with items left inside the boat in the bilges, but it would be prudent to empty all the lockers to avoid the possibility of burst baked bean cans etc! Even at a safe temperature the hull laminate will be slightly softened and it is important to provide extra support, ideally in the form of a pur-pose-built cradle or legs secured to strong points on the deck. I have found that the safe distance from the hull to place the lamps is about four feet, but this will be governed by the temperature in the workshop and the type of reflector.

Depending upon the shape of the hull, one lamp will heat about three square feet, but from a practical point of view several lamps are required to cover as much of the hull as possible at one time. In prac-tice, boatyards buy six to eight lamps, since they consume 1,500 watts each (at 240 volts), and the number is therefore limited by the capacity of the electrical wiring in the workshop. Ideally they should be sup-ported on robust, height-adjustable stands, as the tubes are very vul-nerable to accidental damage. Equally, if the hull is not heated up sufficiently (below 40°C) the drying process will be minimal and all you will gain is a large bill for electricity..!

The time taken to dry out a hull has been dramatically reduced by this method and on average it takes around four days for each section covered by the lamps, although sections of an older saturated hull can take as long as two to four weeks.

Another, slower, yet effective method of drying is with the aid of a

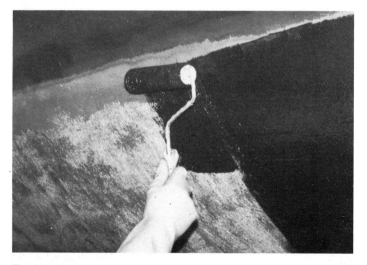

The following sequence of six photographs shows rebuilding a hull with epoxy paint and filler. **1** Here the first coat of epoxy paint is worked well into the exposed laminate

2 The hull is fitted with epoxy filler

3 The filler is abraded to a smooth fair surface

dehumidifer. This is a mobile unit available from most hire shops, which can be plugged into an ordinary domestic electrical supply and is often used by builders to dry out plaster in new houses. It is placed under the boat and the bottom is completely encapsulated within a polythene skirt, from the hull topsides to the ground, which is also covered with a plastic sheet. This method of drying can take as little as two to three weeks, instead of three months or more in a heated workshop. With all methods of drying it is important to keep the bilges warm and dry and to drain water tanks, to reduce the chance of condensation forming on the outside of the hull.

When the hull is dry, as measured with a moisture meter, the epoxy paint system can then proceed. The first coat is worked well into the exposed laminate. Following this, the hull is reprofiled with epoxy filler. When smooth and fair, sufficient coats of epoxy paint are applied to give a total dry film thickness of about $^{24}/_{1000}$ inch (600 microns) – roughly equal to the gel coat it replaces. Finally, the anti-fouling or primer is applied, at the timing specified by the paint company.

This treatment assumes that the hull is sound under the gel coat. I have already described the procedure for removal of deep seated blisters, but where wicking has been left undetected or unchecked for several years, the delamination and deterioration can be extensive. There can also be extensive deterioration by hydrolysis where the hull is wet, but there are no apparent blisters. In such cases, the deteriorated and delaminated sections should be cut back to sound material and relaminated using glassfibre cloth and a vinylester or epoxy laminating resin. When the resin has fully cured, it must be coarsely abraded and degreased to give a good mechanical bond, and then you proceed with filler and paint as before.

Another way to rebuild the hull is to apply a sprayed lay-up using a chopper spray gun with vinylester resin (see page 4). This would certainly be easier than applying glass fibre cloth upside down, to the underside of hulls. However, a greater thickness will be required to achieve the same strength as a woven cloth. The chopper gun is also an expensive piece of equipment, for use only by skilled operators.

Inside of hull

Having protected the outside of the hull, what about the inside? Although I have no firm evidence of blistering caused by water working its way though from the inside of the hull, it is important to seal the bilges, and again, epoxy paint is the ideal coating. I have seen water in the bilges cause slow disintegration of the laminate by hydrolysis. This is obviously more likely where the inside of the moulding is dry and resin-starved. Fortunately, most moulders apply a thick coating of resin or gel coat on the inside, known as a 'flow coat', to reduce the ingress of water. However, those areas which are difficult for the laminator to reach are often the very areas where bilge water lies.

4 A further coat of epoxy paint is applied. Note the hull support on the left of the picture. These should be designed to support the hull on the topsides, leaving the underwater area completely clear

5 Further coats are applied using alternate colours to provide a visual aid so that no areas are missed. If the coating is damaged at a later date it is also possible to see how many coats are damaged

6 After the final coat, anti-fouling and boot-topping paint is applied

It is also important to prevent water from seeping into a moulded keel which has internal ballast. If this is steel or cast iron it can swell up as it corrodes, straining and possibly fracturing the moulding. Also, once water has found its way into a keel moulding, it is then trapped. Hydrolysis is a very slow process and it may take 10–15 years, but because the breakdown of the laminate is from the inside outwards it will not normally be noticed until a leak develops.

I remember one particular 15-year-old boat where I noticed a pinprick of rust in the layer of anti-fouling on the keel section. On investigation I found that this rust was coming out through the moulding, from the inside. As I removed a section of gel coat a small trickle of water ran out. The glassfibre laminate was wet and mushy and could be picked away with ease. Behind this was what could only be described as a pile of rusting scrap metal, although the ballast was specified by the builders as being one section of cast iron. Water had been seeping into the keel over the years and all that was holding some areas together was the outer layer of gel coat.

Detection

Those owning or thinking of buying a glassfibre boat will naturally want to know if blistering exists. I am commonly assured by proud and careful owners that their hulls are blister-free and that they check them each year when applying a fresh coat of anti-fouling paint. I am afraid that

Glass fibre cloth being laid up onto a hull with epoxy laminating resin, to restore the original strength (see page 38)

only fairly advanced blistering is visible through a layer of paint, particularly where there are several years' build-up or it is uneven.

The only way to check for the early stages of blistering is to remove small sections of the anti-fouling two or three inches square (50–75 mm), being careful not to damage the surface of the gel coat. If no blisters are immediately visible, minute ones can be detected by running your eye along the hull, so that the light is reflected off the gel coat. If the lighting is poor, or your eyesight bad, it is possible to take a rubbing of the area which will often show up any imperfections.

If blisters are found it should be possible to determine the type from the descriptions given here, but it is well worth paying a qualified yacht surveyor to examine the hull in more detail, to determine the extent and severity. Based on his findings, he can also recommend the best form of repair and in the long term this could save money – if too little gel coat or laminate is removed it may result in further blistering, and if too much, you may be going to unnecessary expense.

Above all else, avoid the 'expert' at the yacht club bar. When the subject of blistering and osmosis is raised there is always too much unqualified free advice available. I have seen a considerable amount of unnecessary damage caused and money wasted, due to irresponsible advice, where a little knowledge has been very dangerous.

I surveyed one particular thirty-two foot sailing cruiser where the owner had been advised that the $^1/_4$ inch (7 mm) blisters were not serious, that he should examine them each year and that if they did not increase in size, he should ignore them. This he had done for six years and the boat was now 15 years old. On examining the hull I found that most of the blisters, which covered about 70% of the underwater area, were around $^1/_4$ inch (7 mm) in diameter. I removed the gel coat from the tops of half a dozen and in two areas the glassfibre laminate underneath was soft and had delaminated. I found that it was so soft that I could push my spike right through the hull. The subsequent repairs included relaminating large areas of the hull and the cost was more than double that of replacing gel coat with an epoxy coating. Had the repair been carried out six years previously, he would almost certainly have saved more than half the cost, plus a saving due to inflation.

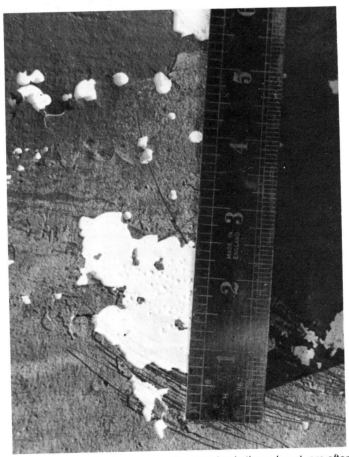

Smaller blisters, like these caused by aeration in the gel coat, are often obscured by the layer of anti-fouling paint

Above and below. These blisters, $^3/_4 - 1^1/_4$ inch (20–30 mm) in diameter, were easily seen without removing the anti-fouling paint. When pierced, pungent, highly acidic liquid squirted out and ran down the hull

1 The gel coat was peeled back to reveal the cavity

2 The acidic liquid within the blister had degraded the resin and glass fibres, which now resembled dried breadcrumbs

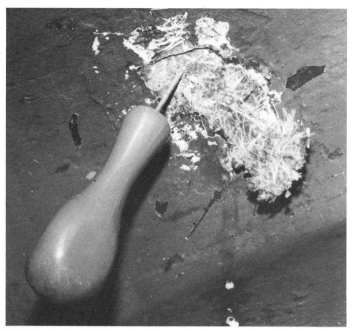

Soft laminate 1 The laminate felt soft when a section of gel coat was removed from this mildly blistered hull

2 So soft that my spike could be pushed through the ¹/₂ inch (13 mm) thick hull with ease

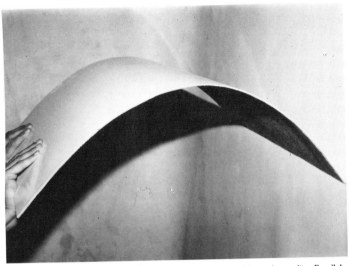

Above and below. This panel of glassfibre laminate is quite flexible (above) but when bent around this simulated plywood bulkhead (1) a hairline stress crack (2) appears in the gel coat

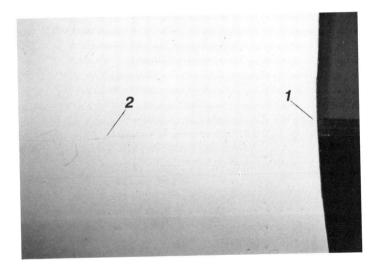

Chapter Three

Hulls

When buying a boat, do you get what you pay for? Or put another way, is a boat at the cheaper end of the market likely to be less robust than one at the top end, which may cost up to twice as much for the same overall dimensions? The answer is yes, normally, but like most things in life it is not quite as simple as that – the upmarket model may have a flimsy hull but a very smart interior with expensive joinery and soft furnishings.

I remember surveying just such a motor yacht – the sort that tends to be labelled as a gin palace. It was very smart with all the most up-to-date electronics, and the interior could not be described in boating terms for it was more like a house, with a full size sitting room, kitchen and three bedrooms all with bathrooms en suite. On the fabric-covered walls were hung oil paintings and there was even a separate library – all this within 55ft (17m). The problems started to mount up when I examined the detail, opened lockers and crawled around the bilges. Steel fastenings were commonplace and rusty, bulkheads (or should that be walls) were interior grade plywood and delaminating, the engine bearers would have been undersize for 50 hp diesel engines, let alone the 500 hp ones fitted. The hull itself was lightweight and poorly stiffened, resulting in numerous stress cracks which would eventually develop into fractures right through the hull. So, although as a general rule a more expensive boat will have more robust mouldings, one cannot assume this and a careful examination of the boat's construction is worthwhile.

Hull construction

Glass fibre reinforced plastic is a remarkably strong material, but it cannot withstand excessive flexing. If it is flexed too much, particularly around a hard spot, it will fracture.

There are several ways of constructing a rigid GRP hull. It could be made very thick, but this would be both heavy and expensive.

Sandwich construction can be used to provide a very stiff moulding, as on many racing boats, but this is also expensive and, under stress or on impact, delamination of the core from the outer or inner laminate is possible. A less common method of hull construction, where foam is injected between the hull and an inner moulding to provide buoyancy, also provides excellent support while the foam remains intact, but it is very difficult to repair due to the inside of the hull being inaccessible. A more common method is to incorporate woven rovings or woven cloth which are considerably stronger and due to the thicker strands of glass fibres, also provide a more rigid laminate than one laid up with chopped strand mat alone. Even with the addition of woven rovings or cloth, a relatively heavy and expensive laminate would be required to obtain the desired rigidity. The most common approach in the 1970s was to lay up a reasonable thickness of chopped strand mat, incorporating at least one layer of woven rovings and rely on the bulkheads, interior mouldings and joinery to support the hull and prevent flexing.

Unfortunately, where a plywood bulkhead, section of joinery or interior moulding is bonded to the hull, it can produce what is known as a hinge effect. Although this can be caused by the mere force of the water on the hull, imagine a situation where a boat is secured to a pontoon, several other boats are moored on the outside in a raft-like fashion, and the force of the wind or tide transfers immense pressure onto one or two fenders between the hull of the inner boat and the pontoon (proportionately, the same applies to those craft sandwiched in the middle). This causes the hull to bend, like a hinge, around the hard spots formed by the bulkheads etc., which normally results in hairline cracks in the gel coat, or even a partially fractured hull.

To overcome this problem, longitudinal stringers are moulded into the hull. These can be made of timber but need only be rigid polyurethane foam formers over which the glassfibre is laid up to provide a box section of the same strength. These are known as top hat section stringers. By placing them at about two foot intervals (600 mm) on the hull, a very rigid and therefore robust hull moulding can be produced, without excessive weight.

In addition to the longitudinal stringers, transverse ones, rather like frames, can also be fitted. If these are positioned in line with the bulkheads the result is an immensely strong hull,

Flexing also has to be prevented around keels, rudders, skegs and engine bearers etc. To do this, longitudinal and transverse stiffeners must be used to spread the load from these areas of high stress. Imagine the loading where the keel joins the hull, with a bolt-on fin keel. This also applies to twin keeled yachts. Many have been damaged because the keels are fitted in a splayed, rather than vertical, fashion, and when they sit in soft mud the weight of the boat forces the keels deeper into the mud which has the effect of wrenching them away from the hull, due to their opposing angles. (see page 88.)

When moored on the inside of several other craft, the wind or tide can place considerable loadings on the small sections of the hull around the fenders (above)

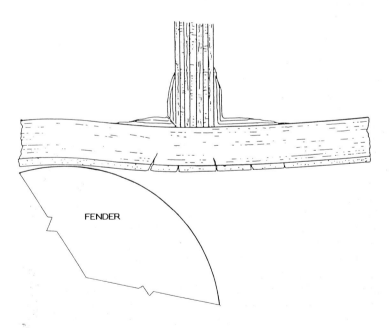

FENDER

The possible result of an inadequately reinforced hull is illustrated above

Hull repairs

Having described how a hull *should* be constructed, it is a sad fact that many are not robust and are all too easily damaged. Of course, even a well constructed hull can suffer accidental damage by grounding or collision, but the extent of the damage will be directly proportionate to the robustness of the mouldings.

It is also a sad fact that, even today, with more small craft afloat constructed of GRP than any other material, many boatyards have insufficient knowledge when it comes to carrying out GRP repairs. Although this sounds surprising, it is also true that many builders of the boats lack the necessary skills when asked to repair one of their own products.

Top hat section stringers – so called because of the shape of the GRP laminate laid up over a foam former

Note the top hat section 'frame' onto which the bulkhead is bonded, thus eliminating any possibility of a hard spot on the hull

Covered here are the most common types of damage and the appropriate repair techniques.

Cosmetic damage

Scratches and abrasions
Every boat will inevitably suffer from scratches and abrasions in the gel coat, particularly on the hull topsides. If these do not extend right through to the glassfibre laminate they can normally be classed as cosmetic.

The difficulty is distinguishing between scratches and hairline cracks. With a light coloured gel coat, the area can be carefully cleaned using a fine brush, such as a nailbrush, to remove dirt from the surface. Any hairline cracks will remain visible, since it will be impossible to remove the ingrained dirt from them. With a dark gel coat, white chalk can be rubbed into the surface and then cleaned off in the same way.

Having satisfied yourself that there are no cracks, the deeper scratches and abrasions can be carefully filled with gel coat resin of a matching colour, as described under star crazing (see page 53–55). I would not recommend this for anything except the deepest areas on boats over two years old, as a line of gel coat with a poor colour match will look worse than the original scratch.

For minor abrasions it is often better to use a mild abrasive compound or even fine sandpaper (1000 grade) to remove, or at least reduce, the visual impact of the damage. With any cosmetic repairs it is worth remembering that the average thickness of the gel coat is only $^{20}/_{1000}$ inch (500 microns) – not much thicker than a postcard. It is therefore important that sandpaper or abrasive compounds are not used too vigorously, otherwise the glassfibre laminate will become visible.

Fading and discoloration
The pigments in most gel coats will eventually fade and the effect will be noticeable more quickly with dark ones like blue, green or red. There are several products on the market which can be painted onto the gel coat to partially restore a faded hull. Also the use of an abrasive compound followed by polish will improve the appearance. Unfortunately there is no long-term solution and eventually the cosmetic appearance can only be improved by painting the topsides.

The same applies to discoloration which normally occurs near the waterline, and is caused by pollution in the water.

Painting
As a general rule, I would recommend that painting the topsides is delayed for as long as possible, particularly on lighter coloured hulls where abrasive compound and polish will remain effective for a longer period. Although it will dramatically improve the whole appearance of the boat, paint is not a permanent solution. Like the gel coat, it can become unsightly due to fading and abrasion. However, having taken the decision, there are coatings available which are more resilient than others and it is well worth paying the extra to have your topsides resprayed with a superior product, which will ensure they remain attractive for considerably longer. One such product is Awlgrip.

Before deciding to change the colour of the boat from, for instance, dark green to white, remember that any deep abrasion is likely to extend through the paint coating to the original gel coat and show up as a contrasting colour.

If the cost of a respray is completely out of the question and your topsides are past the stage of restoration with polish, do not despair. It is quite possible to obtain a perfectly acceptable finish by painting the hull yourself, using one of the modern polyurethane yacht paints. The reason for a DIY repaint being inferior to a professional respray is the unsightly brushmarks it leaves, particularly with the darker colours.

A friend of mine had spent all his available capital on an old, but sound, thirty-four foot sailing cruiser. Unfortunately the dark blue topsides were deeply scratched and had an unsightly streaked appearance where the gel coat had faded. Although he had decided to accept this until he could afford a respray, I suggested that he tackle the work himself, and apply five coats of gloss paint, after filling, fairing and undercoating the hull. This he did, and took as much care as possible to avoid prominent brushmarks. I had advised him not to worry about these, but to give me a call two weeks after completing the coating, when it had fully cured. I arrived at the boat armed with plenty of 800 and 1000 grade sandpaper, which we used wet, to rub down the whole of the topsides and remove the brushmarks. A buffing attachment was fitted to a large right-angled grinding tool and the hull was polished with a mild abrasive cutting compound, of the type normally used on car paintwork to restore the shine. After the application of boat polish, two days' work had transformed the brushmarked paint finish into a gleaming surface, superior to most spray-painted hulls. The only drawback is that the more durable scratch-resistant paints are not suitable for application by brush and in any case they are so hard that they could not be rubbed down in the way I have described. Nevertheless, an additional couple of coats applied in the same way every three or four years will maintain a smart appearance.

A modified form of gel coat which can be sprayed, is being offered by a number of boatyards as an alternative to painting. This has the advantage of being much thicker and more durable than paint, similar to the original gel coat. However, care has to be taken in its application and I have seen such coatings craze after just 12 months. It is also likely that darker gel coats will fade more quickly than the better quality paints, such as Awlgrip.

General maintenance
Abrasive compounds, often known as boat cleaners, are available together with boat polish in most chandlers. Annual use of the cleaner and frequent polishing will maintain the gel coat and help retain the shine for much longer, in the same way as it does on a car. Only pure wax polishes should be used, as those with silicone and other additives will permeate into the surface and impair the adhesion of any gel coat repairs, or paint coatings.

Gel coat crazing

Almost every form of stress and impact to a GRP laminate will result in at least some crazing in the gel coat.

Crazing can take several forms but consists of hairline cracks in the gel coat which are not always easily visible until ingrained with dirt.

Star crazing
Star crazing usually occurs when the laminate is knocked with a sharp object and the hairline cracks radiate out from the point of impact in a

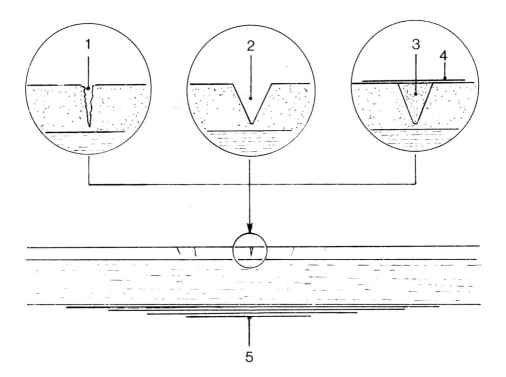

Gel coat crazing. Most forms of crazing in the gel coat which do not extend into the glassfibre laminate can be repaired by opening up the hairline crack (1) into a V-shape (2), filling with matching gel coat resin (3) and covering with Sellotape (4). If the crazing covers more than a few square inches it is likely that the laminate has been weakened, even though no fractures are visible. To overcome this and prevent the crazing from developing again in the weakened area, the inside of the hull must be reinforced with several layers of glassfibre laminate (5), each being smaller in size to form a tapered edge.

Note: A purist would claim that successive laminations on a repair, or bonding of a bulkhead should increase and not decrease in size, (see above). However, as chopped strand mat is normally used, if adequately consolidated, it should become one homogeneous layer with no evidence of individual laminations which can ultimately delaminate. Where woven reinforcement is used, it would be important to apply the shortest lamination first and then gradually increase the sizes to form a taper.

ABOVE: Blisters up to 2 in (50 mm) in diameter are easily visible on this hull and have been caused by the advanced stages of osmosis (see page 15)

BELOW: Where the anti-fouling paint has been scraped away to reveal the clear (unpigmented) gel coat, the unmistakable signs of wicking (fibre aligned blisters) are visible where the individual strands of glassfibre have swollen up and broken away from the resin (see page 20)

In this more unusual case of osmotic blistering, the blisters extended from the gunwale as
shown above, down to the waterline, as seen
below (see page 23)

ABOVE: After removing the blistered gel coat from the underwater area, it is important to clean away all traces of acid. Many boatyards have pressure washing equipment such as this, which is ideal because an integral heater will raise the temperature of the water to boiling point (see page 35)

BELOW: It is vitally important that the underwater area of the hull is dry before an epoxy paint coating is applied. Here a Sovereign capacitance-type moisture meter is used to take comparative readings each week, until a figure of between 2 and 5 is reached on the relative scale (see page 28)

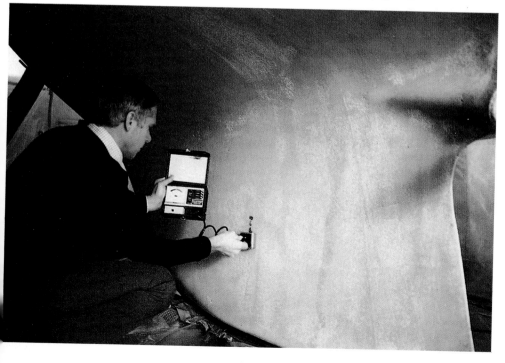

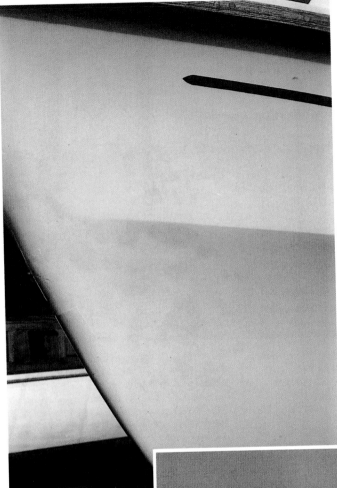

A common failing when carrying out repairs to impact damage, as on the bow of this vessel, is that areas of stress crazing are overlooked as can be seen in the close-up photograph below (see page 53)

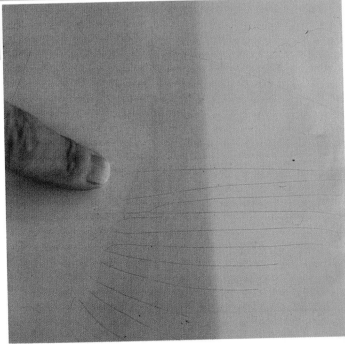

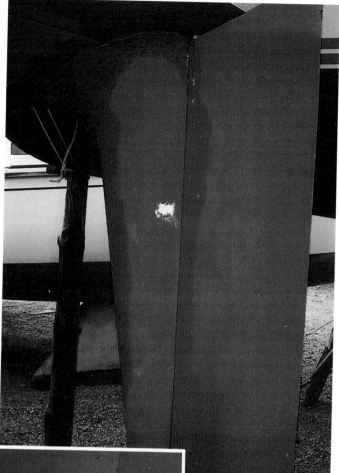

Parallel cracks in the anti-fouling paint are the first warning sign that the hull, or in this case the skeg (right), has been strained. In the close-up below, the hairline stress cracks are visible in the gel coat and were subsequently found to extend into the laminate (see page 53)

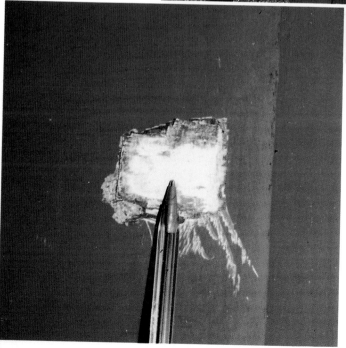

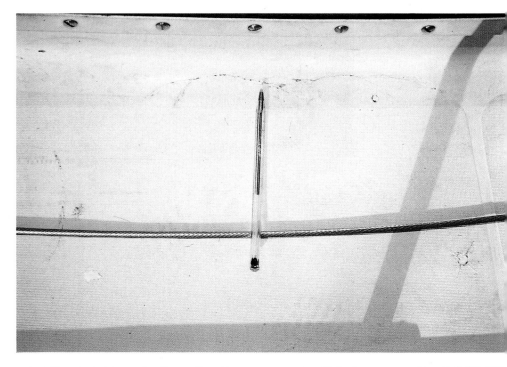

ABOVE: The sandwich construction on the side deck of this yacht has delaminated, allowing the deck to flex and fracture along the inboard edge (see page 75)

BELOW: Water has managed to reach the steel and cast iron ballast encapsulated in this GRP keel, which has not only caused extensive corrosion but has also started to degrade the keel laminate from the inside (see page 40)

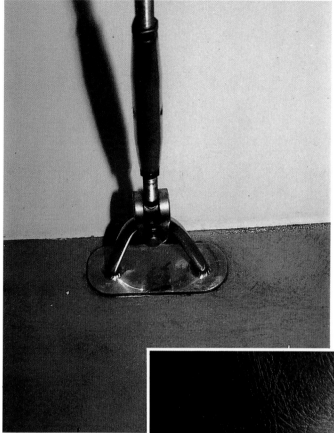

Illustrated above is the commonly used U-bolt type of shroud attachment. This is more than adequate if fastened through onto a bulkhead or similar strong point by means of right-angled brackets, as shown below (see page 83)

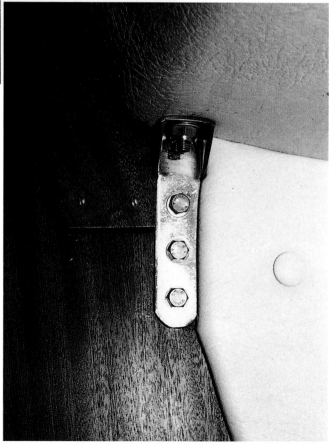

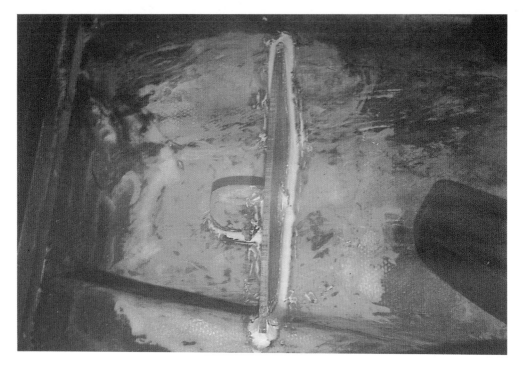

Where the leg of the P-bracket extends up inside the hull, it is important that it should have transverse stiffening. It is relatively straightforward to fit a piece of plywood as shown above, and then bond over both the plywood and P-bracket with GRP laminate to form a secure structure, as shown below (see page 93)

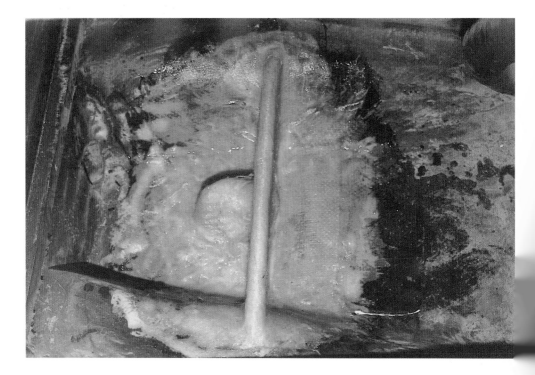

star shape, like the spokes of a wheel or a spider's web. It can also be caused by the hull flexing around a corner of internal joinery, or by poor moulding techniques.

Unless the crazing is very severe, with the gel coat breaking away, it is unusual for the glassfibre laminate to be damaged. To check this, the surface can be tapped with the edge of a coin and there should not be a dull or hollow sound. A repair can be effected by carefully opening up each crack into a V-shape by using a pointed metal instrument such as a small chisel or even a screwdriver.

Wash the area with fresh water and when completely dry, mix up some gel coat resin, using exactly the right amount of catalyst. Care should be taken not to mix it too vigorously and introduce air bubbles. Fill each crack until flush and place a piece of Sellotape or Cellophane™ over the top. Firstly, this excludes the air which would otherwise prevent a full cure and secondly, if just the right amount of gel coat is used it is possible to obtain a smooth finish which requires the minimum amount of abrasion and polishing. If the repaired area does need to be rubbed down when cured, use only a very fine wet-or-dry sandpaper (used wet, 800-1000 grade). This can be followed by a mild abrasive compound such as metal polish.

With any gel coat repair the most difficult task is to obtain a good colour match, even with white. As a general rule, try to obtain the resin from the boat's original manufacturer. With a colour other than white, it may appear to be dark at first, but in time should fade to a better match. If you insist on a matching shade immediately it will eventually fade and show up as a lighter patch. A perfect colour match is almost impossible except on a fairly new boat, and with a darker colour such as red, blue or green, painting is the only answer if a larger area has to be repaired.

Hairline stress cracks

Individual cracks, or those running in parallel lines in the gel coat, are very common due to the flexing or panting of the unsupported areas of the hull mouldings. They are often found along hard spots such as bulkheads, but impact can cause them almost anywhere.

On one particular thirty-five foot sailing cruiser which I surveyed, I discovered extensive stress crazing in the midship sections, both to port and starboard. The hairline cracks were very difficult to distinguish as they were relatively new and were not yet filled with dirt, which would normally make them stand out against a light coloured gel coat. I asked the repair yard to carefully remove the gel coat from the visibly crazed areas, to see whether they extended into the glassfibre laminate. With the aid of a bright light on the inside of the hull one could easily make out the fine hairline fractures extending up to $1/8$ inch (3 mm) into the moulding. I then asked for the gel coat to be removed at the top and bottom of the vertical crazing to determine its full extent. To cut a long story short, when we had finished, we ended up with three

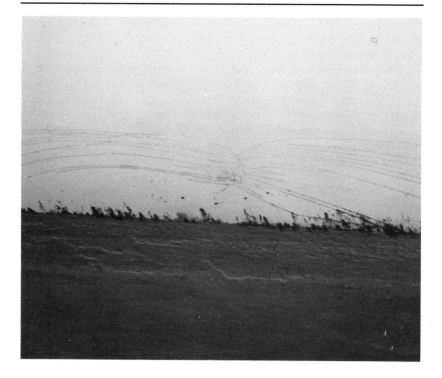

This area of horizontal stress crazing is particularly vulnerable to ingress of water, being just above the waterline. The hull has flexed around the top of the berth moulding which was slightly flexible except where a part bulkhead is fitted (centre of crazing)

almost circular areas of crazing about 4 ft (120 cm) in diameter on both the port and starboard sides. The hull had flexed in the areas bounded fore and aft, by bulkheads and top and bottom, by the gunwale and berth moulding. On questioning the owner, it was eventually discovered that while the cruiser was moored to the quayside the previous weekend, a gale had forced many other craft to seek shelter and moor on the outside of her. The gale lasted most of the following night and the pressure of at least eight vessels on the outside of her had caused the damage, as the fenders had been placed midway between the bulkheads.

Because, as in this case, fractures are often difficult to identify in the glassfibre laminate, some means other than the naked eye is required. One very efficient, and sometimes alarming, method is to use a penetrant stain, similar to that used to detect faults in metal castings. Alternatively, if the inside of the hull is accessible and unpainted, a bright light will highlight the cracks if the gel coat is removed from the damaged area. Failing this a strong magnifying glass can be used.

Having identified the fractures, the damaged areas must be cut back to sound material. This is most effectively done by using a coarse grinding disc on a small right-angled electric grinding tool. A shallow taper should be ground back from the fracture at an angle of about 5° in all directions.

The prepared surface must be washed, degreased and dried out thoroughly. The area can then be rebuilt with glass fibre cloth and resin. In highly stressed areas, it is advisable to use a vinylester or epoxy resin, in preference to polyester resin. Both epoxy and vinylester resins have far superior adhesive qualities and will therefore provide a more effective repair, particularly on an older boat. Using a polyester resin, (the one the hull was moulded with) will not provide 100% adhesion.

Unfortunately, at present, pigmented epoxy gel coat resins are not available and most epoxy laminating resins cannot be exposed to sunlight, as they suffer UV degradation. For this reason, conventional polyester resins or vinylester resin should be used for repairs to the hull topsides where a gel coat resin finish is required. When using polyester, it is important to choose a superior isophthalic one, and with vinylester resin, a special matched polyester gel coat will be required.

On underwater and other painted surfaces, the epoxy resin repair should be sanded down to a smooth, slightly hollow finish and sealed with a generous coat of epoxy resin or compatible epoxy paint. When cured, this can be lightly sanded, degreased and over-coated with anti-fouling primer, followed by anti-fouling paint.

Where polyester or vinylester resin is used, again the repair should be sanded to a smooth, slightly hollow finish and then coated with gel coat. As mentioned already, matching the colour is difficult. It is also difficult to obtain a smooth, pinhole-free surface. A great deal of patience is required in sanding, filling, and sanding again, until a smooth surface is obtained. It can then be polished with a mild abrasive compound.

One important point to remember when using epoxy laminating resins, is that chopped strand mat with an emulsion binder cannot be used, as the epoxy resin will not dissolve the binder. In this case, a powder-bound chopped strand mat must be used. In any case, this is a better alternative for use below the waterline.

Having completed the repair on the outside of the hull it is important to strengthen the inside, because even where no fractures are visible, the flexing or panting necessary to cause crazing in the gel coat will almost certainly have weakened the hull, if only by a minute amount.

Strengthening can be done by laying up three or four layers of 1½ oz or 2 oz (450 gm or 600 gm) glass fibre CSM or cloth in the damaged area. Alternatively, a stringer or stiffener can be fitted to prevent flexing on large unsupported panels. These can be formed by laying up three or four layers of CSM or cloth over a rigid polyurethane foam stringer of about 3 ins x 1½ in (75 mm x 40 mm) to form what are known as top hat section stiffeners, due to the shape of the laminate formed over them. The exact dimensions will vary according to the size of boat and the

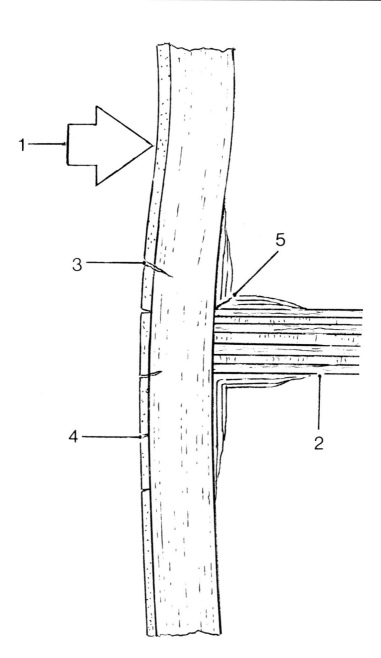

Repairs to partial fractures. 1 The impact or loading (1) on the hull causes it to bend around joinery (2) or an interior moulding and this will often cause a fracture extending into the glassfibre laminate (3) as well as crazing in the gel coat (4) and cracked bonding on the inside (5)

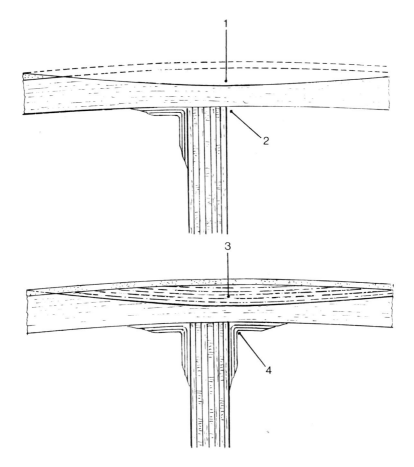

2 To effect a strong and lasting repair the fractured area should be ground back (1) and the cracked section of bonding removed (2). The area is rebuilt with glassfibre laminate (3) and, if on the topsides, coated with gel coat. A new section of glassfibre bonding is applied (4)

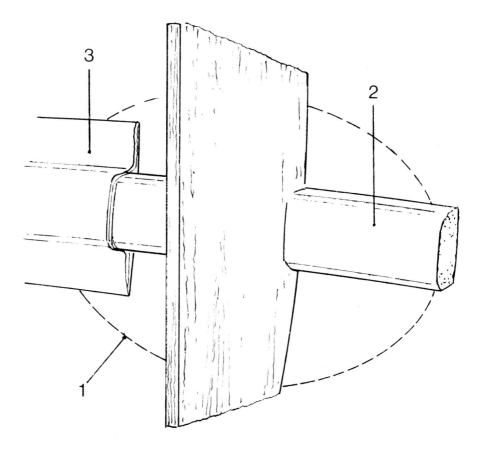

3 A top hat section stringer should be fitted on the inside of the hull across the area of flexing (1). A foam former (2) is used, over which successive layers of glassfibre are applied (3)

area to be stiffened. Again, epoxy laminating resin should be used for preference.

Power boats

Stress crazing and fractures are very common on the V-shaped spray rails often moulded into the hulls of power boats. Because of their shape they are able to withstand only slight flexing before they fracture. Indeed they are often relied upon to provide stiffening to the hull. The tremendous loading placed on them when pounding into rough seas at over twenty knots is more than all but the most robust hulls can withstand.

Crazed gel coat was removed from the spray rail on this power boat and a fracture right through the hull was uncovered

Cracks are found in line with any hard spots behind the spray rail and also along the angle formed with the flat section of the hull. On a boat capable of high speeds, any stress cracks are dangerous and, if left, can quickly develop into a fracture right through the hull. Repairs are carried out in the same way as already described, but the fitting of internal stringers is imperative in the areas of identified weakness.

I recall a 45-foot motor yacht which was taken out on sea trials after the owner had fitted additional fuel and water tanks. On his return later that day he reported that she was performing well and was still able to maintain 23 knots in rough conditions. However, could I investigate a slight leak which had developed? After checking the stern gear and seacocks I noticed that water was trickling down from underneath the new tanks fitted beneath the forward berths. My immediate reaction was that the water tank was leaking but, on tasting the water, I found it salty. I then discovered that there were small fractures in the spray rails along the line of a bulkhead. The reason was that the two new tanks, one for water and one for fuel and each with a capacity of about 50 gallons (228 litres), had been inserted between existing bulkheads, to which they were fastened, with no other form of support. Almost half a ton was distributed along two $1/2$ inch (13 mm) strips of the hull, at the base of the bulkheads. It is not difficult to imagine the pneumatic drill effect when driven into rough seas at 23 knots.

Extensive damage

Where the hull is completely fractured or holed, a repair is relatively straightforward, from the point of view of strength. The problems normally arise when trying to rebuild the original shape of the hull.

I surveyed a 29-foot motor cruiser which had one side damaged beyond repair when she was driven ashore in a gale. This side of the boat was cut away and discarded. A new side was laid up in the original mould, slightly oversize. This new section was offered up to the boat and cut to size. The edges on each side of the joint were tapered on the inside and then joined together with an ample build up and overlap of glass fibre CSM and cloth, using epoxy resin. That boat is now almost as strong as she was prior to being damaged.

Most damage is not quite as extensive as that, but even with a fractured area a few feet square, restoring the hull to her original shape is not easy. If the original mould is accessible it is often worthwhile to use this, even for a relatively small repair, but when it is not, it may be possible to make a small mould of the desired section on a boat of the same class. Failing this there has to be a compromise.

Firstly, the damaged area should be cut out completely, whether holed, or only fractured. (It is common for stress cracks to radiate out several feet from the point of impact and this should be checked in the way already described.) The inside and outside edges are bevelled to form a pointed V-shape around the edge of the hole, with the taper on the inside much shallower than that on the outside. The inside of the hull, surrounding the hole, must be coarsely abraded and degreased and, if painted, all traces removed. A polished sheet of Formica or painted plywood is then screwed or bolted to the outside of the hull ensuring that it is a good snug fit around the edges of the hole. Ideally, short self-tapping screws are used to minimise subsequent filling.

Working from the inside, a release agent is applied to the Formica or plywood, followed by gel coat resin of a matching colour. A layer of glass fibre tissue is laid up, followed by layers of 1¼ oz or 2 oz (450 gm or 600 gm) of CSM or cloth to match the original lay-up, all wetted out with resin. Ensure that the first layers are carefully stippled into the outer tapered joint.

As mentioned on page 57, at the very least a superior isophthalic polyester resin should be used and in highly stressed areas, a vinylester or epoxy resin. In the case of the latter, it is also important to remember that emulsion bound chopped strand mat must be substituted with a power-bound variety.

If the Formica or plywood has been secured with fastenings right through the hull these should be removed after the repair is built up flush with the surrounding hull and has been left to cure for 24 hours.

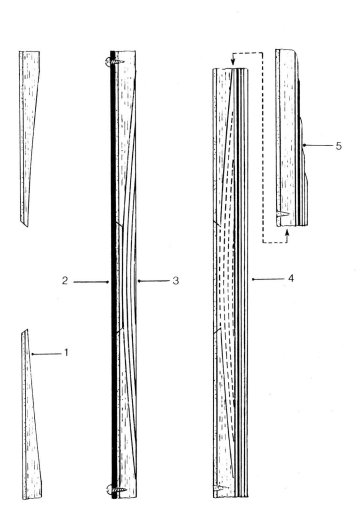

(1) The damaged section of the hull is completely cut out and the inside of the hull ground back on a shallow taper. (2) A sheet of Formica or plywood is screwed to the outside of the hull to act as a mould and the hull is rebuilt from the inside (3). (4) Remove the Formica or plywood mould and fill the screw holes. A reinforcing laminate is laid up across and overlapping the repaired area with tapered edges (5)

The holes can be veed out from the inside and filled with CSM.

In either case, a layer of CSM followed by woven rovings is laid up to overlap the repair by about two feet, or to adjacent joinery or mouldings. If these are closer than one foot (30 cm), on anything but a small repair they should be removed prior to commencing and replaced afterwards. Over the woven rovings, apply three layers of CSM. Each successive layer of glass fibre must be smaller in size, to form tapered edges, and thus avoid any hard spots. If the area is bounded by mouldings or joinery they should be tapered back from this point.

When cured, any rough edges can be sanded down on the inside and the area painted or linings replaced. The holes on the outside are filled with get coat resin.

On the subject of curing, temperature is very important and, as a general rule, the repairs should be allowed to cure for two weeks at 68°F (20°C) before launching. A temperature close to this must be maintained immediately prior to, during and after carrying out any repairs with polyester resin. Higher temperatures will reduce the curing time.

With epoxy resins, the temperature range is more flexible as long as it is suitably high after completion of the repair.

With all resins, the exact temperatures and curing times will depend upon the type of catalysts and accelerators used and the manufacturer's instructions must be studied carefully before use.

Internal damage

When the hull suffers external impact, or even flexing and panting, this often causes damage on the inside. It is therefore important to check the glassfibre bonding of joinery and mouldings to the hull. It is common for this to crack along the right-angle joint with the hull or to pull away from one of the surfaces.

If stringers or stiffeners are fitted these should also be checked for cracks or movement.

In addition to checking the inside of the hull in the area of damage or flexing, it is important to check at least 6 ft (1.8 metres) on either side. The opposite side of the boat may also be damaged if a bulkhead, joinery or moulding is fitted across the hull, since any impact will be transmitted through it.

When repairing internal damage, the surrounding area must be abraded, cleaned, degreased and any paint removed to provide a good mechanical bond. The cracked or loose glassfibre should be replaced using an epoxy laminating resin. This is particularly important on bulkheads or other areas of timber, where the adhesive qualities are superior to polyester resin. In fact the reason for glassfibre bonding pulling away in the first place is often due to poor adhesion. Where teak-faced plywood has been used, the teak veneer should be removed as the natural oil in the wood will impair the adhesion.

Where a hull relies on the support of the internal structure, one loose

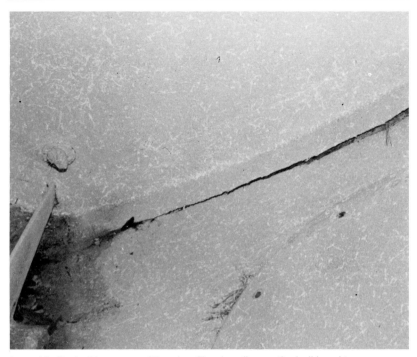

Impact to the hull has caused the glassfibre bonding on the bulkhead to come away from the hull

or cracked section of bonding is not dangerous in itself. However, it does put additional strain on the bonding to the hull fore and aft of the damaged section and can cause a chain reaction if not repaired.

Sandwich construction

Sandwich construction is almost universally used on deck mouldings, to stiffen the flat horizontal sections, as described in the next chapter.

On hulls, it is commonly used to provide a strong, yet lightweight moulding. In Europe it is most often found on racing yachts, where weight is all important, but elsewhere around the world, it is widely used on cruising yachts, both power and sail.

The basic principle is that a relatively thin inner and outer GRP skin, with a rigid core material in between, produces an 'I' beam effect, which is both strong and lightweight. This is the principle in theory. In practice it is not always possible to maintain perfect adhesion between the inner and outer skins and the core material. The core is normally end grain balsa or rigid foam. On racing yachts, good adhesion is obtained by a vacuum bagging technique, where the three components are drawn together under a vacuum pressure. On cruising yachts, it is currently

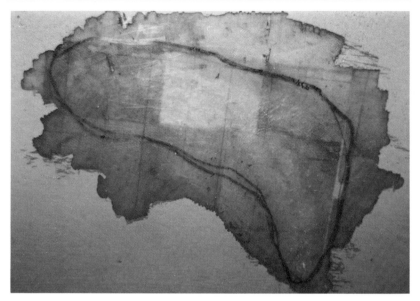

Delamination on a balsa cored hull. The anti-fouling paint has been removed from the underwater area of a hull moulded with clear (unpigmented) gel coat. The blocks of end grain balsa core material are visible. The area of delamination is circled in black

unusual for such techniques to be used. The result is that voids remain between sections of the core material and the GRP skin. Due to the way most hulls are built in a female mould, it is usually the joint between the outer skin and the core which has most voids.

At sea, particularly in rough conditions, the loading on the outer skin can cause the bond between the core and the skin to break away around the perimeter of each void. This can gradually grow into larger areas of delamination. Since the sandwich construction relies upon the bond between the three components to provide its strength, once the bond is broken, it becomes weak. Panels that have been affected will flex and eventually fracture.

The other major potential problem is that if the inner or outer skin is punctured, water will enter the core and collect in the voids. Where end grain balsa is used, it will gradually degrade and no longer provide support for the skins, which will once again flex under load. It has also been found that many types of foam will degrade if left water-logged for long periods.

This form of sandwich construction should not be confused with the use of balsa or foam on the inside of a conventional solid laminate hull, where it is used to provide stiffness and insulation. On such a hull, a thick outer laminate will be found, with a thin inner laminate to retain the core material.

Delamination on a foam cored hull. A three inch (75 mm) hole was cut through this foam-cored hull to identify the type of damage. A fracture was found in the foam and delamination from the inner skin. Note how thin the inner and outer skins are, making them vulnerable to puncture by a sharp object

Repairs

In the early stages of delamination, this can often be repaired by injecting epoxy resin into the voids, as described on page 75. However, regardless of the size of the delamination, if water has penetrated the core, all wet areas of balsa or foam must be removed. This entails the removal of the inner or outer skin throughout the affected area.

To effect a satisfactory repair, the area must be thoroughly washed and dried and new core material bonded in place with a core adhesive, using a vacuum bag. A new inner or outer skin is then laminated in place, with a 12:1 taper around the edges. Ideally, the laminate should also be vacuum bagged.

The above procedure should be carried out only by skilled operators under controlled conditions.

Chapter Four

Deck and coachroof

The majority of deck mouldings now incorporate the coachroof and cockpit, as well as hatch openings and winch pads etc. It is therefore more complicated than a hull moulding. Until the deck moulding is fitted to the hull and supported by bulkheads, this complex structure is relatively flexible and crazing can occur due to mishandling as well as stresses set up during the moulding process.

When examining crazing – hairline cracks in the gel coat – it is important to determine their cause. It is not always possible to be certain, but there are usually some indications.

Latent crazing

If the cracks form along a corner in the moulding, for example, between the deck and coachroof or where the cockpit coaming joins the coachroof, they may have been caused during the movement or fitting of the mouldings to the hull. If the deck does not quite fit, it may be clamped down into position causing distortion. Eventually cracks can form along these corners. Another very common area for cracks to occur is between the cockpit coamings and the gunwale where there is a narrow strip of side deck.

In general this type of crazing is not serious, since it rarely extends into the glassfibre laminate. It can often be repaired successfully by vee-ing out the individual cracks and filling them with gel coat resin. To confirm that it does not in fact extend into the laminate, the gel coat should be removed completely, across at least one of the major cracks.

Stress crazing

More serious crazing can be caused by flexing, due simply to walking on the moulding, or by stress from a deck fitting. This can also occur almost anywhere including the corners in the moulding.

A deck moulding after being removed from the mould. Note the complexity, with recesses for the windows, raised sections for the grab rails and an anchor locker on the foredeck. Also note how vulnerable it is without the support of the hull and bulkheads

Where flexing is the cause this should be fairly obvious because the moulding will feel flexible underfoot. I recall one such 28-footer with extensive hairline cracks which the builder put down to moulding stresses. After his men had been down to the boat for the third time, to fill the same cracks which continually reappeared, I was called in and diagnosed flexing, due to insufficient stiffening.

The horizontal surfaces are usually reinforced either with stiffeners moulded to the underside or by the use of sandwich construction, with a core of balsa or foam. The flexing normally occurs where the stiffeners are of inadequate size or spacing, or because the sandwich construction does not extend to the whole of the horizontal surface area.

In both cases the only long-term solution is to bond in additional stiffening under the deck.

The other common cause of crazing is deck fittings with insufficient backing pads or plates under the deck, but this is covered in the next chapter.

The following 5 photos show repair to deck fractures. **1** Stress cracks were visible in the gel coat on the deck. Small sections of gel coat were removed and the cracks were seen to extend into the laminate

2 The whole area was ground back to the depth of the cracks, which extended about ⅛ inch (3 mm)

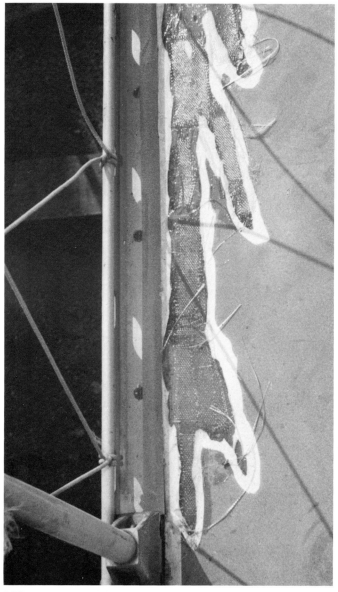

3 The area was rebuilt with glass fibre cloth and epoxy laminating resin

4 The surface was abraded and filled with epoxy resin filler

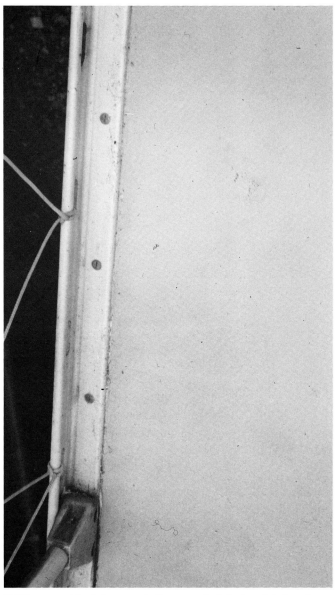

5 This was rubbed down and after a coat of deck paint, the strong invisible repair was complete except that the underside of the deck was reinforced to prevent further flexing in the future

There is little point in repairing stress crazing without eliminating the cause, but once this is done, repairs are carried out in the same way as described on the hull.

Sandwich construction

Although a balsa or foam sandwich is the best way of achieving a rigid yet light moulding, it does have its drawbacks. The fact that it is a sandwich creates the possibility of delamination. However good the bond may be between the glassfibre laminates and the core material, there is always a weakness if the moulding is overstressed.

On boats built in the late '60s and early '70s sandwich construction was relatively new and it is not uncommon to find delamination in highly stressed areas. Of course, it is also possible on later boats due to human error or extreme loading. The first signs are usually a distinctive crackling sound underfoot. Eventually crazing appears in the gel coat, on what is now an unsupported area.

Assuming that it is not so severe that the sandwich has to be cut open and rebuilt, a fairly successful repair can be effected by injecting resin assuming that the core material is dry. This is done by drilling holes at three inch intervals (75 mm) in the area of delamination. Epoxy laminating resin is then mixed with a slow catalyst to prevent an exorthermic reaction and injected using a large hypodermic syringe, without the needle. Working from one edge of the delamination, sufficient resin is injected until it emerges from the adjacent holes. When the syringe is removed, a small wooden plug is inserted into each hole to ensure that the resin penetrates the whole area. After the injecting is completed the plugs are removed. When the resin has cured the holes are carefully filled with matching gel coat resin. If this is too unsightly due to a poor colour match, or is within a non-slip pattern, it may be possible to camouflage it with deck paint.

Two points to remember, then, are firstly to fit a depth gauge on the drill to ensure that the holes pass through the core material but not the lower laminate, and secondly not to exert too much pressure on the syringe, otherwise the resin may force the moulding into a hump.

Although the sandwich could be injected from below, thus preventing an unsightly repair in the gel coat, I would not normally advise this, as gravity will ensure that it is both difficult and messy.

Blistering

I have encountered gel coat blistering caused by both osmosis and wicking on deck mouldings, but it is rare. It has normally occurred where a pool of water has been allowed to remain for long periods when a boat has been laid up ashore.

If it does occur it is usually a cosmetic, rather than structural, problem but is more difficult to repair because the finished appearance is

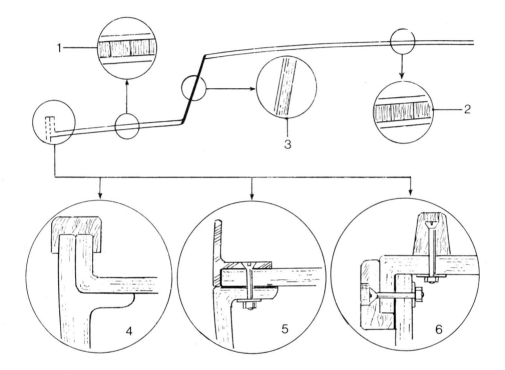

Deck moulding and hull to deck joint. Most deck mouldings have balsa sandwich construction on the decks (1) and coachroof top (2) as well as other horizontal areas such as the cockpit seats and sole. The vertical sections like the coachroof sides (3) are normally solid glassfibre laminate. The most common types of hull to deck joint are: (4) where the deck sits on a deck shelf and an upstand forms a bulwark with a timber capping. (See previous photograph of deck moulding.) (5) An alloy toe rail covers the joint. (6) A flange on the deck fits over the hull and a timber rubbing strake covers the joint

more important above than below the waterline. Small random blisters can be opened up, washed out and filled with matching gel coat resin.

More extensive blistering will require total gel coat removal in the affected areas, which will have to be reprofiled with filler and then painted to match the gel coat as closely as possible. Depending upon where the blistering has occurred, it may be possible to coat the areas with deck paint. I would not recommend recoating large areas with gel coat, as obtaining a smooth pinhole-free surface would be very difficult, time-consuming, and therefore exorbitantly expensive.

Hull to deck joint

In the early days of GRP boats it was fairly common for the hull to deck joint to leak and, in some cases, come apart. These days such occurrences are less common, except where rigging is inadequately secured, as described in the next chapter.

The type of joint it is will obviously have a bearing on its integrity. Many builders have devised complex and very secure joints, but basically, as long as a sealant is applied between the two mouldings and they are securely bolted together, there is little possibility of them separating under normal conditions.

In the past, no sealant was used and the joint relied mainly on glass-fibre bonding over the inside of the joint and a rubbing strake fitted over the outside.

As already mentioned, polyester resin does not provide a perfect bond, and moreover, a few layers of glassfibre applied over the joint are rarely waterproof.

As the inside of the joint is often obscured by linings, it is best to check around the outside for any signs of movement, particularly at the stem, where it has been known for the deck to peel open like a banana.

Cosmetic damage

The advice given in the previous chapter, on cosmetic damage to hulls, applies equally to the deck moulding.

However, due to the larger number of sharp bends and corners, small voids are quite common. These normally occur immediately beneath the gel coat because it is difficult to laminate the relatively stiff glass fibre mat around the complex shapes and particularly into tight corners. It is like trying to hang wallpaper on an awkward surface and tease out all the air bubbles from behind it.

Where the gel coat is left unsupported it is as brittle as an eggshell, and moderate pressure will expose any voids. If the glassfibre laminate underneath does not appear dry and resin-starved, the opened void can be filled with gel coat resin or, if more than $1/8$ inch (3 mm) deep, with epoxy filler with gel coat over the top.

Larger voids, covering several square inches, either immediately beneath the gel coat, or within the layers of glassfibre laminate, should not be opened up. It is easier and neater to drill holes and inject epoxy resin, as described for delamination on sandwich construction.

Another common fault is caused by aeration in the gel coat. A mass of tiny voids appear and become unsightly because dirt remains trapped in them. This occurs particularly where a non-slip pattern is incorporated as it is very difficult to brush gel coat into the mould without causing aeration in these areas. A satisfactory repair is almost impossible where extensive small voids or pinholes occur. The normal compromise is to paint the sections with deck paint or to fit a deck covering such as Treadmaster.

The number of voids found on a deck moulding are a good indication of the quality. Not only does a careful laminator create very few voids, but a reputable builder thoroughly checks all the mouldings with a rubber hammer or similar tool to find any defects, and repairs them before the boat leaves his yard.

I recall one dissatisfied boat owner who was so annoyed at the number of gel coat defects on his new cruiser that he demanded a replacement or his money back. Three months, several letters and one survey report later, he had another boat and this time with completely unblemished mouldings. It proved that the builder in question, who had a poor reputation for quality, was quite capable of producing satisfactory mouldings when pressed.

If the moulding on an older boat has deteriorated to such a degree that it needs to be painted, the abrasion resistance of the paint coating is even more important than on the hull topsides, due to people walking, jumping and dragging all manner of gear across it. The horizontal sections subject to the most wear are best covered with non-slip paint, which can be repainted or at least touched up each year. Alternatively a very durable covering, such as Treadmaster, can be used.

Chapter Five

Fitting out

With the transition from timber to GRP construction, the same principles were not always applied when attaching fittings to the new material. This was often because builders who, having had no training or background in boat building, thought they could get rich quickly in this new, easier method of construction.

Being a much thinner and more vulnerable material, it needs to be supported and stiffened in areas of stress just as much, if not more, than timber. Even today some basic rules are overlooked, which results in failure, or damage occurring.

After surveying a well-known class of offshore cruising yacht, I mentioned in my report that the stemhead fitting, to which the forestay was attached, was fastened to the deck with no bracing to the hull. My client telephoned the builders who assured him that they had built a considerable number of this class and never experienced a problem. That satisfied him. Two months later he and his wife set out into the Atlantic and on the second day were heading into a force eight gale, under storm jib. They only became aware of a problem when water started rising over the cabin sole. On investigation, water was found pouring into the forepeak and they eventually realised that the foredeck had lifted away from the hull. Despite lowering the jib, water was still coming in faster than it could be pumped out and they took to the liferaft. Luckily a ship picked them up the following day and they lived to tell the tale. The attachment of the forestay was of particular importance on their next boat!

Rigging attachment

Forestay attachment
The attachment of the rigging at deck level is of paramount importance, as can be seen from the graphic example given above, and as a general rule fastening should never be to the deck without some form of direct bracing to the hull or a substantial bulkhead. Most stemhead fittings

On this stemhead fitting, note the substantial plate which runs down the stem, through which it is fastened. There is no possibility of the fore-deck being lifted by the forestay

Even if there is no obvious crack in the deck, the first signs of move-ment can be detected by laying a straight piece of wood on the deck. The hump was immediately apparent here – note the gap under the far end

incorporate a plate running down the stem, through which it is fastened. Had this been the case in the example I recounted, all would have been well. Alternatively, some forestay plates are fitted aft of the stem with a tie rod bracing them from the underside of the deck, to a strongpoint on the hull.

Inner forestay

Whether the inner forestay attachment is for a cutter rig or an emergency forestay, it is equally important. It is not advisable to rely upon the strength of the foredeck alone and ideally the load should be transferred through to a strong point. This can often be achieved by using the bulkhead at the aft end of the chain locker, as shown in the diagram on page 83, for shroud plates.

Babystay

The amount of load from a babystay will depend upon the size of the yacht and design of the rig. Wherever possible the babystay should be braced through onto a bulkhead, or a beam which will spread the load transversely.

However on many designs, it is common to see distortion in the coachroof top around the babystay plate. This will often distort the aluminium alloy frame of an adjacent forehatch, so that leakage occurs around the seal. On some designs, the load is taken through on to an adjacent bulkhead. This is fine in principle, but on a number of French yachts in particular, the minor bulkheads are not secured at the base, but merely slotted into an internal sole moulding. The result is that the load from the babystay plate lifts the bulkhead, leaving a gap between the base and the cabin sole.

Designers – or is it the builders? – do not appear to consider the all important mast and rigging when designing the interior layout. Priority seems to be given to finding room for the extra berth or a toilet compartment.

On many designs, the only way to provide support for the inner forestay plate is by fitting a removable strop from the underside of the deck or coachroof to a strong point on the hull. I say removable, because it need only be in place when sailing.

Shroud plates

Shroud plates are equally important and ideally the yacht should be designed so that the cap shrouds line up with the main bulkhead, to which they can be directly secured by slotting through the deck, or by some form of brace or bracket under the deck.

Part bulkheads or knees under the deck are ideal fixing points for the lower shrouds so long as they are large enough and adequately bonded to the hull. On some designs the load from the shroud plates is taken by strops or tie rods fitted from the underside of the deck down to strongpoints on the hull. This would be fine if the points were in fact strong.

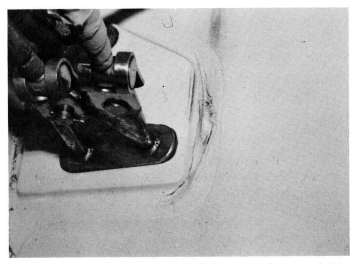

Above and below. Fractures in the deck inboard of this shroud plate (above) had been filled with gel coat, but reappeared because inadequate reinforcement was provided under the deck (below). The stainless steel backing plate is bending under the load, causing the deck to deform into a pronounced hump

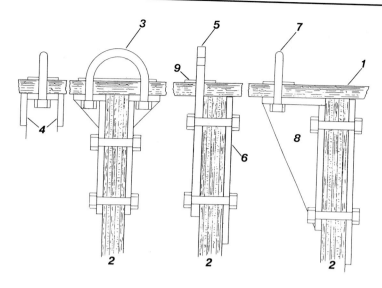

Shroud plates. The load placed on a shroud plate cannot normally be sustained by the average deck moulding (1). This load should be transferred to a transverse bulkhead (2) or a substantial plywood knee securely laminated to the hull.

A U-bolt (3) can be fitted above a bulkhead and fastened to right-angled brackets under the deck, fabricated from stainless steel. These are through-bolted to the fore and aft sides of the bulkhead. Triangular webs are welded across the angle to provide a rigid bracket, as shown in the side view (4).

A conventional chain plate made up from a flat bar of stainless steel (5) can be slotted through the deck and fastened to a bulkhead. Note the substantial backing plate (6) fitted on the reverse side. Where a shroud plate is up to six inches away from a suitable bulkhead – shown here as a U-bolt fitted transversely (7) – a larger right-angled bracket can be fabricated, incorporating larger triangular webs (8).

In order to prevent leaks, U-bolts incorporate sealing plates. With a chain plate, a small stainless steel plate (9) can be slotted over the top with bedding compound beneath it

I know of at least two popular classes of boat where the owners have complained to me of slack lee shrouds under sail, no matter how much the rigging is tightened. I found that the hull was being deflected inboard by the tie rods from the shroud plates, due to the enormous loading on them. On an average 30-footer this can be as much as three tons.

If shroud plates are to be braced to the hull, the attachment point must have substantial longitudinal and transverse stiffening to spread the load. A plate simply bonded to the hull moulding is not sufficient.

Backstay attachment

Backstay plates do not normally present a problem and are often fastened directly to the transom. If U-bolts or plates have to be secured to the deck, then additional reinforcement or adequate bracing is required beneath the deck.

If in doubt about the integrity of rigging attachment points, for instance for shrouds or inner forestays, a straight edge can be placed fore and aft on the deck and this will show up any pronounced hump, if the moulding is beginning to lift. This is usually followed by crazing around the fitting or even a fracture right through the moulding.

Mast support

It follows that if the rigging induces enormous loads, then so too will the base of the mast, except that this will be a compressive load.

I have heard many builders and owners extol the virtues of the keel-stepped mast as opposed to the deck-stepped mast and I agree that, in theory, it should be a stronger arrangement. This is true with timber construction where the mast normally rests on one of the strongest points of the hull, but with GRP it is not necessarily so, particularly on a fin and skeg design, where the mast step is placed on the relatively thin shell of glassfibre, which may coincide with the forward end of the keel.

To visualise the loads being placed on the hull, imagine the mast standing on the intersection of two planks of wood, placed on the ground in a '+' shape. For the sake of this example the centre of the planks would be secured to the ground to provide the same effect as a ballast keel. Attach the rigging to the ends of the planks and apply the loads experienced when sailing. As you can see, the planks would have to be very thick, or reinforced in some way. Bearing in mind that the hull of an average 30-footer ranges in thickness from around $^3/_8$ inch (9 mm) at the gunwale to a maximum of one inch (25 mm) at the keel, considerable stiffening is required to sustain these loads, and prevent twisting or distortion.

I encountered a common problem when called in to investigate why the owner of a 28-foot sailing cruiser could not close up the gap between the forward end of his cast iron fin keel and the hull. He was convinced that the keel bolts had failed. I discovered that the base of the keel-stepped mast had distorted the hull by three inches and because it was now misshapen, the top of the keel did not fit. Had the owner looked at the glassfibre bonding on the bulkhead and joinery in the area, he would have noticed gaps and cracks where the hull had been forced away from it.

As can be seen, keel-stepped masts require substantial transverse and longitudinal strengthening to spread the load. If it is not possible to tie this in with the main bulkhead, to which the cap shrouds are also attached, then a steel framework can be bonded in, onto which the mast is stepped and the shrouds are attached by tie rods, to equalise the two loads, rather than transmitting them through the hull – remember the planks. On many racing yachts where the designers are aware of the hull's limitations, metal space frames are fitted to the inside of the hull to accommodate the keel, mast and rigging loads, including the fore and backstays.

With deck-stepped masts, distributing the load can be easier if, once again, a substantial main bulkhead is placed under the mast step and incorporates the cap shroud attachment. If a post or pole is fitted under the coachroof to transmit the load from the mast step to the keel, then of course the same conditions apply as with a keel-stepped mast.

Keels

After giving a talk at a local yacht club which covered damage caused by grounding, I was approached the following day by a very worried owner who had touched the bottom in his long-keeled cruiser a few months before. Over the intervening weeks, he had noticed water in the bilges, but had put it down to a leaking stern gland. My talk had caused him a sleepless night and he arranged for the boat to be hauled out so that I could examine her. I found that the aft end of the keel had been fractured at a point where a bilge water sump had been formed between the aft end of the ballast and an integral fuel tank. Water was therefore seeping into the sump. It was also found to be seeping into the integral fuel tank, albeit at a slower rate, but this would have caused the engine to fail in the very near future. Keels of whatever configuration, rarely suffer from structural failure under normal sailing conditions, but problems do occur when grounding, both intentionally or by accident, that's what pinpoints the weaknesses.

Long traditional keels
A long keeled hull often incorporates the keel within the hull moulding, with ballast fitted inside and encapsulated in resin – a form of construction which is normally very strong. Any form of grounding damage will be confined to the point of impact and rarely results in damage caused by stress loadings elsewhere.

If a vessel grounds heavily on rocks or a similar hard object, it is quite possible to fracture the hull moulding and allow ingress of water into any voids around the ballast. It is therefore most important that any such damage is dried out and properly repaired, as soon as possible. If not, water can migrate throughout the ballast, where there are bound to be small cavities. Drying out such cavities can be both difficult and time-consuming. If the ballast consists of steel or cast iron, there is the possibility of further damage caused by corrosion.

Some long keeled designs have the cast iron or lead ballast fastened externally to the base of the keel. In general, this tends to be a very strong form of construction, with the added bonus that the ballast will

On this boat the ballast keel is attached to a short stub moulded integrally with the hull. A mast support transfers the load from the underside of the coach roof, down to the hull at the forward end of the keel stub. No floors or other form of transverse stiffening was fitted and the combined loads and stresses resulted in a fracture across the hull, on the lefthand of the picture and a crack running along the radius between the hull and the keel stub

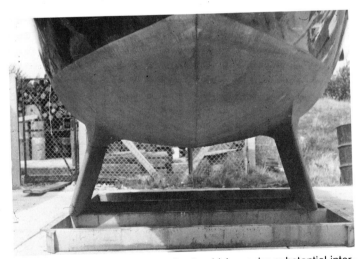

Note the opposing angles of the keels which require substantial internal reinforcement to withstand the wrenching force if they sink down into mud

often take any grounding impact and prevent damage to the hull moulding itself.

Moulded fin keels

Again, the fin keel is moulded integrally with the hull and ballast is
inserted from the inside. As well as being vulnerable to damage at the
base, this form of keel construction relies heavily on the strength of the
hull moulding around the root of the keel and the amount of reinforcement on the inside of the hull, in the form of floors and other stiffening.

A common occurrence is where grounding impact to the base of the
leading edge of the keel causes damage to the hull around the top of the
trailing edge, together with damage to the internal structure, including
the floors and joinery. It is therefore important to ensure that the hull is
adequately reinforced, particularly over the after end of the keel. Many
prudent owners, especially those with more lightly constructed performance yachts, have had additional or new, more robust floors fitted
over the keel, particularly after a small amount of movement has been
detected.

Externally fastened fin keels

The most common form of fin keel on modern sailing yachts, are made
of cast iron or lead and are fastened externally to the hull moulding.
These have the advantage that in a minor grounding incident the keel
itself is unlikely to be damaged, apart from superficial scratches – or
dents in the case of lead. Once again, it is the strength of the internal
reinforcement that is important. In addition, the keel bolts and particularly the strength of the hull around the keel bolts will be tested. Ideally
there should be large backing plates under the keel bolts on the inside
of the hull, to spread the load over a larger area. Some designs have a
fabricated steel or aluminium alloy structure, through which the keel
bolts pass – which in turn will often be incorporated into a more elabo-
rate structure which will also take the mast and rigging loads. Another
popular form of reinforcement is top hat section mouldings, often incorporated into the interior bunk and sole moulding, which act as stiffeners or floors where they run across the top of the keel. However for
many years one mass production yacht builder incorporated such a
moulding, but instead of fastening the keel bolts through the lower
flanges of the top hat sections, they insisted on inserting the keel bolts
on the adjacent unsupported area of the hull. Not surprisingly, it was
common to find gaps forming between the hull and top hat flanges adjacent to the keel bolts.

Moulded twin keels

'Twin' or 'Bilge keeled' yachts have keel structures similar to fin keeled
yachts, but of course there are two of them. Where the keels are
moulded integrally with the hull, they can suffer grounding damage to
the base of the keels, but since they tend to be much shallower than fin

The backing plates under the keel bolts are far too small – only fractionally larger than the bolt heads – and the transverse stiffeners are not carried across the keel

The keel has larger backing plates, but the hull, laminate was not strong enough to prevent the keel from being ripped out when driven onto a lee shore

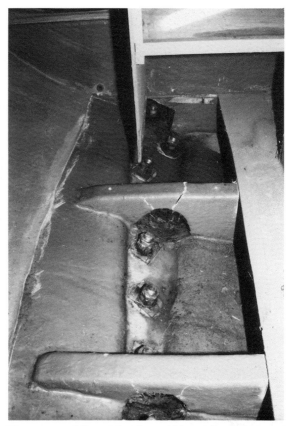

The structural 'floors' fitted over this externally fastened twin keel was weakened at the time of manufacture by the semi-circular cut-outs on the undersides. When over-stressed, the floors fractured at the weakened points

keels, there is less loading on the hull over the aft end of the keels.

Externally fastened twin keels

Cast iron twin keels, fastened to the hull externally, are the most common configuration. Twin keels are often attached to the hull at opposing angles, so that they will be more or less vertical when the yacht is heeled, thus providing a better sailing performance. This presents a major potential problem when drying out on an uneven bottom, or in mud, because there is a tendency for the keels to be forced apart and some craft have actually had a keel completely wrenched off, when moored in a mud berth. In most cases, this has been due to inadequate hull thickness around the keel bolts and/or reinforcement of the hull in way of the keels.

Repairs

All the types of damage described here can be repaired and grounding damage will often be covered by the vessel's insurance policy. However if the damage has been caused by a weakness in the original construction, an insurance policy may at best cover only a proportion of the repair costs. If indeed there is a weakness, then in addition to completing the repair it will also be necessary to strengthen the hull and/or add reinforcement around the keel.

Prevention

Prevention is better than cure – and certainly much cheaper. But how do you know if the structure over the keel is weak? Simple, you ask a surveyor to examine it – but before calling one in, there are a few simple checks you can make. Is the hull adequately reinforced over the keel(s)? If so, is there any evidence of movement between the hull and the reinforcing structure? On a twin keeled yacht with splayed keels, the amount of reinforcement and any evidence of movement is more important, particularly if the vessel is kept on a drying mooring. Also, check for movement between externally fastened keels and the hull. After any grounding incident, however minor, check for damage to the base of the integrally moulded keels and around the root of the keels, for any signs of movement both on the inside and outside of the hull.

Rudders

Most GRP rudders are made in two halves, the joint being around the outer edge. Sandwiched in between is the stock, commonly a bar of stainless steel or bronze. On to this, inside the blade, smaller rods or bars are attached at right-angles and then bonded to one half of the blade, before fitting the other half on top. Unfortunately these can become corroded or detached and allow the blade to swivel around the stock, with the resultant loss of steering. In this situation, the rudder has to be removed, cut open and rebuilt.

There is at least one well known class of offshore cruising yacht where the rudder stock extends about 3 in (75 mm) into the rudder blade, is bent through 30 degrees and extends for a further 9 in (230 mm). This rudder stock is then bonded to one side of the blade without the benefit of any additional rods or bars. Not surprisingly – and bearing in mind that many of these yachts are used for ocean cruising – the stock eventually works loose.

A more common failing, is for the two halves of the blade to partially separate along the joint, particularly on the leading edge adjacent to the rudder stock. This can normally be repaired by grinding back the edge to provide a good key and then reinforcing the joint with strips of glassfibre cloth or tape, two or three in (50–75 mm) wide.

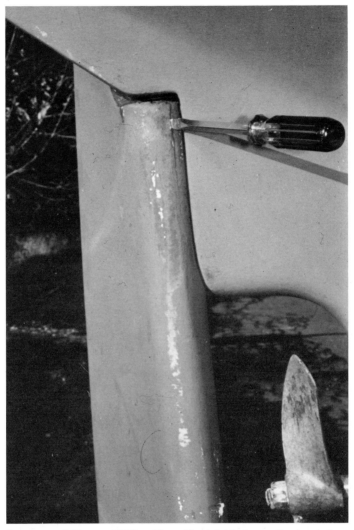

A common failing on GRP rudders. The joint between the two halves of the blade comes apart along the leading edge

One half of rudder blade in the mould. The rudder stock with substantial webs welded to it has been bonded to the blade with GRP laminate, before the other half of the blade is fitted on top

Stern gear

Although stern gear is common to all vessels, not just GRP, it is an often neglected area due to the low maintenance benefits of a GRP vessel.

Shaft brackets

Where a vessel does not have a suitably shaped keel or skeg, a bronze or stainless steel bracket or strut is required to support the aft end of the propeller shaft. Those with a single leg attached to the hull are known as 'P-brackets', since they roughly resemble an inverted 'P', the eye of the 'P' being the hole for the shaft. Those with two legs are 'A-brackets', again because of their resemblance to an inverted 'A'.

The manner in which these are fitted is crucial, due to the sideways thrust they have to withstand. Most of us have experienced the 'paddle wheel' effect of the propeller which has the infuriating habit of pulling the stern away from the quayside or pontoon as we come alongside. When you consider that all this sideways thrust is being transmitted

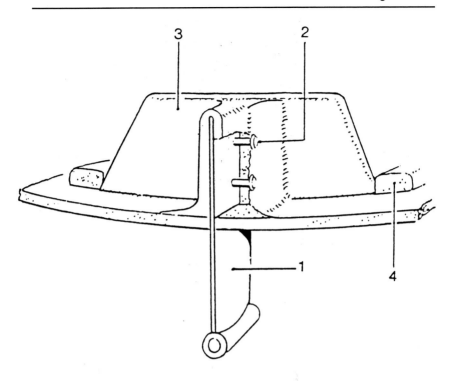

If the single leg type of P-bracket is used (1), it should be securely bonded in with bolts (2) through the glassfibre bonding. A plywood web (3) should also be bonded in, terminating at top hat section stringers (4)

through the bracket, it is obvious that it requires substantial support. Obviously an A-bracket provides better support, particularly if large internal pads are provided for the fastenings, plus longitudinal or transverse stiffening. They are certainly recommended where engines in excess of 50 hp are fitted.

P-brackets having only a single leg are more difficult to fit in such a way that they remain rigid. Those with a flange that fastens to the outside of the hull are best, so long as sufficient internal stiffening is provided. However, the trend on many sailing cruisers is to use the universal type with no flange, but with a long leg, or strut, that passes through the hull and is bonded in with glassfibre laminate on the inside. A great attraction of this type to boat builders is that it simplifies the engine installation and minimises the amount of lining up necessary.

I know of one 32-foot sailing cruiser fitted with this type of P-bracket whose crew, after a five-hour passage under power, noticed some vibration. This became progressively worse, so they stopped and one member dived over the side, thinking that something had fouled the propeller. Nothing was found. Following another half an hour's motor-

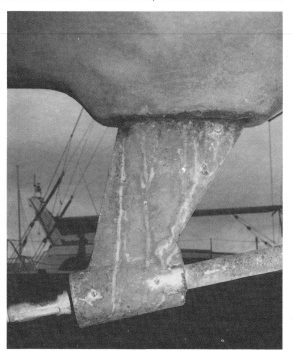

When this P-bracket was pulled from side to side, water ran out from the aperture through the hull

ing, at a slower speed, there was a rattle and a thud and the engine stopped. On entering the cabin to check the engine, water was found to be over the cabin sole and rising. After putting out a 'May day' call, a fishing boat picked them up and managed to keep the boat pumped out until they reached port. When she was lifted out of the water it was found that the P-bracket had slowly worked loose and was eventually wrenched out, leaving a ragged hole in the hull. Luckily a bulkhead had reduced the amount of water which could enter the cabin.

If this type of P-bracket is used, a substantial amount of glassfibre laminate must be applied on the inside, plus at least two fastenings and a plywood web to provide support. Otherwise, the enormous loading will work the bracket loose with eventual leakage – or possible disaster.

If in doubt about one which is already fitted, additional stiffening can be fitted. I have also found that it pays to apply some glassfibre reinforcement around the joint on the outside of the hull. To obtain adhesion to the metal shaft, an epoxy resin should be used. Not only will this strengthen the bracket, but it will also prevent ingress of water, which is very common around the slot through the hull.

Checking a P-bracket for movement is ideally carried out immediately after the vessel has been lifted from the water. By pulling the bracket

Note the crack indicating movement where this single leg type of P-bracket passes through the hull

This boat was lucky not to suffer more extensive damage when the P-bracket broke off without warning and the propeller hit the hull

sideways and up and down, the smallest amount of movement will be evident as water will escape from the aperture through the hull.

Propellers

Propellers come in various shapes and sizes and can be fixed, folding or feathering. Although they are available in bronze, aluminium alloy and stainless steel, the most commonly used material on conventional stern gear is manganese bronze. This is really a fancy name for high tensile brass, being a 60/40 alloy of copper and zinc. The biggest drawback with this material is being prone to galvanic corrosion, in the form of dezincification, particularly when connected to a stainless steel shaft. Dezincification is exactly what the name suggests: galvanic action creates an electrical current between the dissimilar metals immersed in salt water (an electrolyte) and the zinc is dissolved, leaving the copper which has very little strength.

A badly dezincified propeller can retain its original shape, but any form of impact, such as a hammer blow during a survey, will cause it to crumble away. Dezincification can easily be identified if the propeller is cleaned and polished. In the early stages the copper coloured patches are highlighted against the original brass colour.

Corrosion can be minimised by a correctly installed sacrificial anode. (Nigel Warren's book *Metal Corrosion in Boats*, Adlard Coles Nautical, covers this subject in more detail).

This dezincified propeller crumbled away when the edge was gently tapped with a hammer

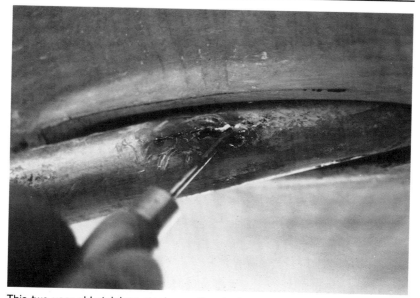

This two year old stainless steel propeller shaft was found to be extensively corroded with only the outer 'shell' intact. No sacrifical anode had been fitted

Propeller shaft

Manganeze bronze shafts were once very common, but they are likely to corrode and are also more prone to wear in way of bearings. More common today are stainless steel shafts, which are less likely to wear. Stainless steel does suffer from pitting or crevice corrosion, where there is a reaction between the different alloys which make up the stainless steel. A good quality stainless steel of a grade similar to 316 should be used. But even this has to be protected by a sacrificial anode.

Tip clearance

A conventional propeller will work most efficiently in solid, undisturbed water. On many vessels the flow of water over the propeller is anything but undisturbed, but without redesigning the hull or skeg immediately forward of the propeller it is difficult to improve it. There is another commonly neglected area and this is the tip clearance, the distance between the tips of the propeller blades and the nearest section of the hull, skeg or rudder. Insufficient clearance will cause cavitation, where water will be disturbed and aerated and the propeller will no longer provide efficient propulsion. One often sees boats in which an original engine has been replaced with one of a larger size, which has a proportionately larger propeller, but with less than half an inch (13 mm) of tip clearance, so that it is impossible to use the extra horsepower.

Above and below. The three-bladed propeller is almost touching the hull at the top. This will cause cavitation and loss of power. Where a larger two-bladed propeller has been fitted, it was necessary to cut away the skeg. In so-doing this will cause cavitation and negate any benefits of fitting a larger propeller

Cathodic protection

I do not intend to cover this vast subject in any detail, but where stern gear incorporates dissimilar metals, or dissimilar metals are used on the rudder and other fittings, protection will be required against corrosion. The simplest way to do this is to fit a sacrificial anode. For a craft in salt water, this will normally be a zinc anode and in fresh water a magnesium anode.

The basic principle is that the anode will corrode before other metals on the hull and can be replaced when necessary. The simplest anodes are those which can be fitted directly to the propeller shaft, but these are small, have a limited life and, as they are eroded they can become loose and rattle around on the shaft. Another, improved type, has a bracket that remains clamped to the shaft even when the anode is completely eroded.

More effective are the larger anodes which are through-fastened to the hull and which must be electrically bonded to the fittings they are to protect. This will normally entail the installation of a bonding wire from the anode fastening on the inside of the hull to the engine. If there is no flexible coupling between the engine and the shaft, this will then provide a connection between the anode, the shaft and the propeller, through the engine. In addition, a bonding wire should be secured to the stern tube and shaft bracket. Flexible couplings on the propeller shaft should be bridged with a bonding wire.

Deck fittings

The fitting which is most often insecurely fastened is the stanchion base. When I consider the leverage that is placed on this fitting by a stanchion around two feet long, it never ceases to amaze me how inadequate backing pads are on many production boats. I know of one builder who experienced so many failures on his boats that he produced a standard repair and reinforcement kit – which he sold to unfortunate owners! Although being fully aware of the weakness, the boats were still built in exactly the same way 10 years later.

I have heard builders say that the stanchions are only designed to take the weight of the crew falling against the guard wires, which are in turn supported by the pulpit and pushpit. However, as we all know, rightly or wrongly stanchions are used as a hand-hold by others when coming alongside, where the leverage is also inboard and fore and aft, not just outboard. A simple way to test the adequacy of stanchion bases is to hold the top of the stanchion and while pushing it inboard and outboard see if the deck flexes. If there is anything more than minor movement, additional stiffening is required.

The ideal backing pad for a stanchion base is ³/₄ in (20 mm) plywood, bedded to the underside of the deck with a layer of glassfibre or resin paste. The pad should extend to the hull side and be at least two inches (50 mm) larger than the base on the other three sides. If the deck is very

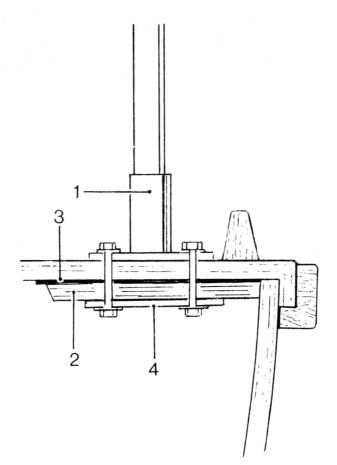

Stanchion bases (1) should be through-bolted onto a plywood pad (2) which is bonded (3) to the underside of the deck. A metal backing plate (4) is fitted under the nuts

flexible a four in (100 mm) overlap is advisable. A metal plate or one in (25 mm) diameter heavy gauge washers should be fitted under the nuts.

Where ordinary washers are fitted onto the glassfibre moulding, without a pad, it is not unusual for these to pull through the deck, causing a fracture which will not only leak, but be very expensive to repair.

A similar problem is common with mooring cleats. Although a backing pad is often fitted, small, standard size washers are used on the fastenings. A timber insert in the sandwich construction is not sufficient on its own, a plywood pad at least 12 in x 6 in (300 mm x 150 mm) is needed on the underside of the deck moulding. Again, a metal plate or large heavy gauge washers are required under the nuts.

With the popularity of anchor lockers in the foredeck, a common failing is to place a mooring cleat too close to the edge of these lockers,

Above and below. The first signs of trouble around stanchion bases
and pulpit feet is stress crazing

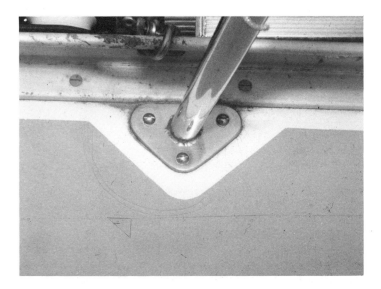

Note how the light gauge washer on the stanchion base has been pulled with ease, through ³/₈ inch (7 mm) of glassfibre laminate without even bending the stanchion

where the deck moulding is weak. In adverse conditions the deck can fracture. With this type of foredeck arrangement the siting of cleats must be given due consideration. This might warrant the resurrection of the old faithful Samson post, which would overcome the problem.

Sandwich construction

In chapter 1 I described how a solid timber or plywood pad is inserted in the sandwich construction where deck fittings are to be fastened through it. Due to inaccuracy when inserting these pads or a change of deck fitting location, it is not unusual to find the two misaligned. When the fastenings are tightened, the sandwich is compressed, crushing the soft balsa or foam core. This is indicated by a hollow in the deck, around the fitting. Once it has happened, the only way to overcome it is to cut the top or bottom of the moulding away, insert a section of plywood and rebuild the moulding. An alternative solution is to drill oversize holes and fit spacers made up from tube cut to the correct length, but I would not recommend this on any fitting which has to take more than a very minimal load.

Hull support

As an apprentice boatbuilder I was always taught to place the shores or cradle supports in line with a bulkhead or other strongpoint, never on an unsupported section of hull. If you walk around almost any boatyard today you will find glassfibre (and wooden) hulls distorted where a large

The tell-tale cracks in the anti-fouling paint show where the hull has been distorted by this wooden shore

proportion of the boat's weight is taken on one or two unsupported sections of hull.

With more sailing boats being stored ashore without unstepping their masts, boatyards quite rightly insist on a cradle being supplied, as shores will often be loosened by the windage on the mast. Unfortunately, a cradle normally has only four supports and even if it is tailor-made, they rarely line up with bulkheads. The boat will often lean to one side and this results in excessive weight taken on one or perhaps two of the supports.

I recall a 36-foot sailing cruiser belonging to the owner of a boatyard. The foreman had supervised the shoring up, with eight shores on each side of the boat. Unfortunately, the two fitted under the stern quarters were taking most of the weight, because the remaining shores had been progressively driven in, lifting the boat up at the bow. The hull was indented by at least three inches around each shore, and when I examined the hull on the inside, it was fractured in both these areas. The owner was not very pleased.

In a way, the owner of that boat was lucky, because the damage was detected. In many cases the boats are relaunched with the owners bliss-

Note the severely distorted hull around this cradle support

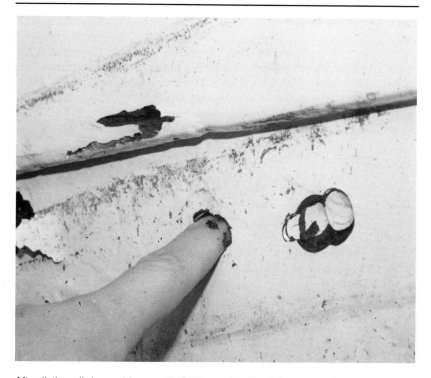

After listing all the problems with GRP construction it is as well to put it back into perspective with this photograph of a wooden fishing boat. It had been in commission up until the time I took this photograph and was so rotten I could push my finger through the planking. A repair was totally uneconomic

fully unaware that even where the hull has not fractured, it has been severely weakened by the excessive localised distortion.

Most yards will check the position of propeller shafts and log impellers etc., before lifting a boat out of the water. If only they took the same trouble when shoring the boat up, damage to the hull could be easily avoided. All they need do is tap the hull with the edge of a coin to locate bulkheads and stringers. With a lightweight hull, where the risk is even greater, bulkheads can often be located by the prominent ridges visible when you run your eye along the hull.

Support is particularly important when a vessel is ashore for long periods, as it would be when fitting out a hull at home. Here, the best method is to use two or more U-shaped supports cut from exterior grade plywood, to fit the hull shape transversely from the centreline up to the waterline. With the hull resting on its keel(s), place one support forward and one aft, if possible in line with a bulkhead or other strong-point. These are then cross-braced fore and aft to hold them in position. The top edge of the plywood should be bevelled to the shape of the hull and a 2 in (50 mm) wide strip of $^3/_{16}$ in (5 mm) plywood fastened to this edge to provide a wider bearing surface. Onto this, some form of padding can, if desired, be attached. If the hull is new I would suggest that the areas under any supports are first coated with epoxy paint. This will not only prevent blistering caused by water retained in these areas, but will also mean that the supports do not have to be removed when applying a protective epoxy paint coating prior to launching.

Chapter Six

How to avoid osmosis and other types of blistering

There are a number of steps that can be taken to avoid the onset of blistering, as outlined below.

Buying a new boat

When buying a new boat, find out what type of resin is used in the hull construction. It should have an isophthalic or isophthalic-NPG gel coat, with isophthalic, bisphenol, or similar resin, used on the first two layers of glass fibre reinforcement (not orthophthalic). Experience has shown that hulls built in this way, under controlled conditions, are much less likely to blister. (See page 25) If the builder does not use this type of resin and refuses to do so on a hull moulded for you, perhaps you should look elsewhere. If this is not practical and the vessel is otherwise built to an acceptable standard, the application of a protective coating is the second line of defence.

Firstly, the hull moulding must be fully cured. With most boat building resins, this can take as long as eight weeks at 60°F (15°C). But check with the resin manufacturer.

The underwater area of the cured hull should be lightly abraded and degreased, so that no gloss or release agent is left on the surface.

Apply sufficient coats of solvent-free epoxy paint to provide a thickness of at least 400 microns. This is normally followed by an anti-fouling primer and anti-fouling paint, but the paint manufacturer's instructions should be followed closely. It is also important to maintain an adequate temperature and not launch the vessel until the coating is fully cured. This is often up to two weeks at 60°F (15°C).

Buying secondhand

If possible, check to see that the hull was moulded using the superior resin systems as outlined above. This will often be confirmed by a low moisture level on the hull, as measured with a moisture meter. If no details are available on the resin used, the moisture levels will still give an indication as to how effective the hull laminate has been in excluding moisture.

If an epoxy coating has been applied, find out whether it was a solvent-free epoxy, who applied it and was it as protection against blistering, or treatment after removal of gel coat. If the coating was recently applied by a reputable boatyard, there may be an insurance backed warranty. The coatings to be suspicious of are those applied to an older boat, by the owner as 'protection'. Firstly, he would have had great difficulty in drying out the hull sufficiently prior to application of the paint. Secondly, it is common to find such a coating applied after discovery of 'minor' blistering.

Where solvent-based epoxy paints are used on older hulls, it is not uncommon for the solvents to migrate through the gel coat and cause a latent osmotic condition to develop into osmotic blisters within 12 months of the application of such a coating.

In all cases, before agreeing to purchase a secondhand vessel – or new – it is prudent to employ a qualified surveyor with a detailed knowledge of GRP construction.

Owning a boat

The first stages in prevention of osmosis are as outlined under the two preceding headings. Assuming that the hull is moulded with a superior resin system, or has an epoxy coating, there are a number of further precautions.

If possible, avoid a mooring where the water is warm or predominantly fresh, as opposed to salt water. (See page 22) If this cannot be avoided, then the type of resin system used or a good protective coating is of paramount importance.

If at all possible, the vessel should be stored ashore when not in use. The benefits here are two-fold, the hull will not be absorbing water during this period and it may even partially dry out. It is no coincidence that those craft left afloat for 12 months every year, develop blisters much earlier.

Do not be put off by those who say that water in the hull will freeze in the winter, causing more damage if a vessel is stored ashore. I have never experienced such damage, although it may be possible in Arctic conditions. It is a fact that glycols are used in the manufacture of polyester resin, including ethylene glycol, which of course, is also used as an antifreeze.

If the hull of a vessel has a thick build up of sound anti-fouling paint, do not be tempted to scrape it all away, back to the gel coat. Not only is this very hard work, but sharp tools can damage the gel coat and most importantly, such a build up actually provides a water-resistant barrier. I regularly encounter cases where blisters appear within 12 months of anti-fouling paint removal.

The fact that there is a thick build up suggests that the vessel is over ten years old and will have absorbed at least some moisture. The amount of moisture may not be great enough for the development of blisters, but it is at a higher level than that recommended for application of a protective epoxy coating – so at this stage a certain amount of protection has been removed and it will not be possible to apply a reliable epoxy coating.

Quick reference section – osmosis questions and answers

During the course of each year I receive numerous phone calls and letters about osmosis. The same questions come up time and again and the most common of these are listed here and, where relevant, there is a reference to the appropriate section in the book.

How many boats suffer from blistering?
My own statistics, based on around 250 GRP craft which I survey each year, show that of all boats between one year and 20 years old, a fairly constant 30–35% have at least some areas of blistering. On boats ten or more years old the percentage increases to around 60%. (See page 22.)

Which areas of my boat should I check for blisters?
Blisters are almost always on the underwater area of the hull or immediately above the waterline. In their early stages they may not necessarily be visible through the layer of anti-fouling paint, so small sections should be carefully scraped off to examine the gel coat underneath.

Other areas include the insides of glassfibre water tanks and anywhere else with a gel coat surface which remains wet. I often find blisters on internal mouldings where water from a deck leak has formed in a pool under a berth cushion. (See page 40.)

Are all blisters found on a glassfibre moulding caused by osmosis?
No, less than half those found are the classic, circular fluid-filled osmotic blisters. The other most common type are caused by wicking (fibre aligned blisters). (See pages 15–21.)

Are boats moored in some areas more prone to blistering than others?
Yes. Areas with fresh water, such as inland waterways, and also the warmer waters of the Mediterranean and Caribbean can cause blisters to form very rapidly. Fresh water has a lower density than salt water and

permeates through the gel coat at a faster rate, and the differential between the fluid within the hull and water on the outside becomes greater and therefore increases the osmotic pressure. Warm water softens the gel coat, making it more permeable, and also speeds up any chemical reactions within the hull. (See page 22.)

Which boats are most resilient against blistering?

It is almost impossible to point to a hull and say whether it will develop blisters. Those constructed to a higher standard with better quality materials are less likely to suffer, but it has to be remembered that each boat is individually moulded and is as good or bad as the laminator working on it. I have often seen hulls with extensive blistering on one side and none on the other, where two different laminators have worked on the hull.

When buying a new boat, you should choose a builder with a good reputation and preferably one who supplies a certificate from Lloyds' or one of the other classification societies. You should also ask what type of resin will be used – there are two basic types of polyester resin commonly used on production boats, Orthophthalic (Ortho) and Isophthalic (Iso). The latter has a far superior blister-resistance than the former. Better again is an Iso-NPG (NPG stands for neopentyl glycol). There are also vinylester and modified epoxy resins, which not only have better blister-resistance but also produce a stronger laminate. One word of warning; if an Iso resin is specified it should be used for at least the first few laminations of the hull and not just the outer gel coat skin. (See page 25.)

Can the colour of the gel coat affect the blistering potential?

Yes. Darker colours contain more pigment and the pigment is less waterproof than the base gel coat resin. Thus, a white pigmented gel coat is more waterproof than a dark blue one. The other problem is that the dark colours tend to be more viscous and retain air bubbles, which are incorporated during the mixing with the catalyst and application to the mould. This aerated gel coat is not only more permeable, but osmotic blisters can form over the voids caused by the air bubbles. The least permeable is an unpigmented (clear) gel coat resin. This has the advantage that any large voids (bubbles or dry patches) can be seen and repaired when the hull is taken out of the mould. (See page 6.)

Blisters have appeared on the underwater area of my hull. Will this have weakened the structure?

Not necessarily. If the boat is more than five years old and the blisters have only just appeared, it is unlikely that the glassfibre laminate has been significantly weakened. In fact, blisters rarely cause any damage. It is moisture which permeates through the gel coat and then leaches out any soluble components, such as unreacted resin and glass fibre binder, to produce an acidic liquid, which degrades the resin and breaks down the bond with the glass fibres, thus weakening the structure. However, in a good quality moulding it is a very slow process and it normally takes many years for any significant weakening to occur.

Nevertheless, like treating rust on steel, it is better to carry out remedial work sooner, rather than later.

NB If blistering occurs in the first two to three years of the boat's life, a more serious defect may exist and it is advisable to seek professional advice. (See page 25.)

I have found blisters on the underwater area of my hull. Should the entire gel coat be removed?

Not necessarily. If the blisters are confined to one or two small sections, the gel coat need only be removed from the affected areas, which are then washed, dried thoroughly and rebuilt with solventless epoxy paint and filler. If the rest of the underwater area is dry (get a surveyor to measure with a moisture meter) it would be prudent to apply a protective coating at the same time. (See page 28.)

But what if the rest of the hull is not dry?

In many cases the rest of the hull is certainly not dry and moisture may well have permeated through to voids and formed a dense solution, but not yet built up sufficient pressure to create a blister – what I call a latent osmotic cell. Even if this is not the case, it is very difficult and sometimes impossible to pull moisture back out through the gel coat when it has taken many years for it to permeate through into the laminate.

The answer to both these problems is to have the hull grit-blasted. A heavy grit, as opposed to fine sand, in the hands of an experienced contractor will pit the gel coat, leaving a cratered surface. The bottom of the craters expose the laminate, enabling it to dry out and the peaks retain the original shape of the hull, so there's no need for it to be completely reprofiled with filler. If the whole surface is cratered this will also open up any latent osmotic cells. (See page 28.)

Should blasting be carried out with or without a jet of water?

I have seen hundreds of hulls which have been sand or grit-blasted, both dry and with the inclusion of water, which is known as slurry-blasting. It appears that if the contractor is experienced it makes little difference. From an environmental point of view there is less dust flying around when water is mixed with the sand/grit. On the other hand, any deeper seated blisters show up as wet patches if dry blasted and these can be opened up at the same time. (See pages 27 and 28.)

A boatyard has estimated to remove the blistered gel coat from my 30-footer and replace it with epoxy paint. If I spend all this money can I be sure that the treatment will be successful?

The short answer is a qualified yes.

In my experience if the gel coat is properly removed, the hull thoroughly dried out and a reliable solvent-free epoxy coating of adequate thickness applied under the right conditions the success rate is around 90%. However, this figure is based on craft treated since 1985 with solvent-free epoxy paints. Those coated with solvent-based epoxies before this date have a lower success rate.

There are, of course, some craft with serious latent defects in the laminate, such as defective resin, where even the best coating applied under ideal conditions will eventually develop blisters on the surface.

I have a ten-year-old boat with no sign of blistering. Does this mean that it will remain blister-free?
No, not necessarily, it might be just taking longer for the moisture to permeate through the gel coat. I have seen blister-free boats, ten or more years old, develop blisters within a year when they are moved to fresh water or warm water.

The moisture content of my hull is very high, but there are no blisters visible. What should I do?
Nothing, at least in the short-term.

As if blisters were not bad enough, we now have something else to worry about – moisture. Years ago we did not have moisture meters to measure the level of moisture in glassfibre hulls and if there were no visible blisters there was no further cause for concern. We have now found that certain types of capacitance moisture meter will identify the presence of moisture in a hull, although they cannot accurately measure the percentage – beware those surveyors who quote percentage of moisture measured with a meter!

Although moisture in a GRP laminate is far from desirable, it does not mean that blisters will necessarily form. I have seen 20-year-old boats where the moisture content is so high that it is off the scale of the meter, but no blisters have developed.

My 30-foot sloop is floating very low on her waterline and a friend tells me the hull can absorb as much as half a ton of water. Is this true?
I hope not, because if so you would have nothing between the inner and outer skin of the hull moulding, certainly no resin. As an example, a 30-foot long keeled hull could probably absorb about 80 gallons of water in the area below the waterline, if it were as porous as a sponge, with no strength and certainly no resin. This would weigh about 7 cwt – well under half a ton. Since a GRP hull contains resin and glassfibre there simply would be insufficient space for such a large quantity of water. Tests carried out indicate a maximum of about 4% water absorption into an average GRP laminate over five years. In other words, the 30-foot hull is only likely to increase in weight by about 32 pounds (14.5 kg) – equivalent to just over three gallons of water.

The reason for the increase in weight is more likely to be extra gear on board and ingress of water into other parts of the boat.

Is it true that water can penetrate the hull from the inside, causing blisters on the outside?
It is unlikely. In theory it *could* occur, but if it were the case I would have expected to see at least one instance where blisters had only formed around the bilge area. To date I have not seen one – but you may know differently ...

The fact is that moisture can permeate through the gel coat at a much faster rate thatn through the whole of the laminate from the inside. Unless, of course, it is a very dry resin-starved moulding. In this case it will be structurally unsound, which is of far more concern that any possibility of osmosis occurring. (See page 42.)

I have applied a protective epoxy coating to my hull. Should I also paint the inside?
In spite of what I said on the previous question, having applied an epoxy coating on the outside, it does make sense to seal the inside, but the hull must be dry – moisture should not be trapped within the laminate. There is also the question of oil in the bilges. This has to be thoroughly cleaned out prior to painting and one could argue that a layer of oil repels the water anyway! (See page 42.)

I have found some small cracks in the gel coat below the waterline, caused by impact. Are osmotic blisters likely to develop in this area?
No. In fact, osmotic blisters are less likely to develop, since moisture can permeate in and out of the cracks without a pressure build-up. But if the area is not dried out and sealed within a reasonable time, it is possible that wicking may develop, though this is a very slow process.

I am worried that one of my through-hull fittings is loose and may be permitting ingress of water into the hull laminate. Could this cause osmosis?
Same answer as on the previous question.

If blistering is such a problem on glassfibre craft, should I buy a timber, steel or aluminium boat?
Timber, steel and aluminium all need constant maintenance, which, if neglected, will have a far more severe effect on the structure over a shorter period of time. A glassfibre yacht can withstand more prolonged neglect for many years without the structure being weakened.

The fact is that all materials require maintenance – wood rots, steel and aluminium corrode and glassfibre hulls may eventually blister below the waterline. But the most important point is that, other than in a few exceptional cases, ingress of moisture and the formation of blisters is a very slow process that takes years, not weeks, to develop.

Glossary

Listed here are some of the more common and possibly confusing technical terms used in this book.

Bond the attachment of two items, but normally means that they are held together by narrow strips of glassfibre and resin laminations i.e. a bulkhead is *bonded* to the hull or the glassfibre *bonding* of the bulkhead to the hull.

Bonded see above.

Bonding see above.

Coachroof not restricted to glassfibre boats, the structure above the deck level often known as the cabin sides and cabin top.

Floor again, not restricted to GRP construction, but often misunderstood. It is a structural member used to reinforce or support the area of hull immediately above and on either side of the keel. It could be constructed of plywood, like a small bulkhead, or of steel, or hollow top hat section glassfibre. The area of the cabin (or cockpit) that you walk on is known as the sole, i.e. cabin sole – never the cabin floor.

Gel coat resin a special resin which can be clear but is usually pigmented and forms the durable coloured surface on the outside of a GRP moulding. Often referred to as gel coat, or gel.

Glass fibre the raw material before impregnated with resin i.e. *glass fibre* cloth.

Glassfibre	when used as one word it normally describes the complete lamination of glass fibres and resin. The same as glass reinforced plastic (GRP).
Glass in	to attach an item to a GRP moulding with laminations of glass fibre and resin. Sometimes known as, to bond in.
Glass reinforced plastic (GRP)	the correct description for construction using layers of glass fibre impregnated with resin, which is commonly a polyster resin.
Laminate, a	successive layers of glass fibre mat or cloth impregnated with resin.
Laminate, to	the process of applying successive layers of glass fibre mat or cloth and impregnating them with resin.
Lay up, a	same as a laminate.
Lay up, to	same as to laminate.
Mould, a	something in or over which layers of glass fibre and resin are applied to produce a GRP moulding.
Mould, to	sometimes used to describe the laminating process.
Moulding, a	any completed lamination of glass fibres and resin i.e. a hull *moulding*
Resin	the liquid plastic material, usually polyester, which is mixed with a catalyst and used to impregnate the glass fibre material, thus producing glass reinforced plastic.
Topsides	not peculiar to GRP construction, but commonly misunderstood. The topsides are the area of hull between the waterline and gunwale.

Index

blistering, 15–46
how to avoid, 107–9
less common, 23–4
detection, 42–6
dry, 19
double gel coat, 19
deck and coachroof, 75–7
prevention, 25–32
treatment, 32–8
bulkheads, 50

cathodic protection, 99
chopped strand mat, 3, 4

deck and coachroof, 68
blistering, 75–7
cosmetic damage, 77–8
hull to deck joint, 77
latent crazing, 68
sandwich construction, 75, 103
stress crazing, 68–75
deck fittings, 99
deck mouldings, 11, 68
delamination, 42

epoxy resin, 57
epoxy paints, 26, 30

gel coat, 3
gel coat planers and peelers, 31, 32
glass fibre materials, 4–6
glass reinforced plastic, 1

grit blasting, 27, 35

hull, 47–67
construction, 47–50
laminate, 8, 10
mouldings, 6, 47
sandwich construction, 65
hull repairs, 50–67
extensive damage, 62
fading and discolouration, 52
general maintenance, 53
internal damage, 64–5
painting, 52
power boats, 60
scratches and abrasions, 51–2
star crazing, 53
stress cracks, 55
hull support ashore, 103
hull to deck joint, 76, 77

interior mouldings, 13–14

keels, 85–90
long, 85
fin, 87
twin, 87, 89

latent crazing, 68–75

mast support, 84–5
moisture meters, 28–9, colour section
mould, building a, 6–11

osmosis
  aeration of gel coat, 18, 19
  dehumidifier, 33, 38
  delamination, 42
  detection, 40
  double gel coat blishers, 17, 19
  dry blisters, 19
  dry voids, 19
  effect of warm and fresh water, 22
  epoxy paints, 26, 28, 30, 38
  gel coat peeler, 31, 32
  grit-blasting, 26, 34
  infra-red lamps, 33, 36
  less common blistering, 23
  moisture meter, 28–9
  prevention, 25–32
  quick reference section, 110–14
  resin types, 25
  statistics, 22
  treatment, 32–8
  wicking, 20–4

plug, building a, 6
propellers, 95–6

shaft, 97

release agent, 6, 12
resin types, 25
rigging attachment, 79–84
  babystay, 81
  backstay, 84
  forestay, 79
  inner forestay, 81
  shroud plates, 83
rudders, 90

sandwich construction, 75, 103
  hull mouldings, 65
shroud plates, 81
stern gear, 92
  cathodic protection, 99
  propellers, 96
  propeller shaft, 97
  shaft brackets, 92–6
  tip clearance, 97
stress crazing, 68

wicking, 21–3